Some Miracles Take Time

• A Love Story • A Tragedy • A Triumph

Art E. Berg

With Reflections by
Dallas Berg

Covenant

Communications, Inc.

DEDICATION

To the three greatest women in my life:

Betty Berg, my mother, for her relentless devotion and limitless sacrifices to the happiness and success of her children.

Rae Howard, my mother-in-law, for her unconditional love and acceptance of a new son.

Dallas, my "forever princess," who has, more than any other person, made the process of time and miracles the greatest experience of my life.

Acknowledgements

Many hands and hearts were involved in the story you are about to share. The task of putting it all to paper would have been impossible without the continuous support and love of family and friends.

I am indebted to those who shared my experiences, whether personally or through the words I have written, and have encouraged this work. They include, Anne Day, Paul and Dawnie Berg, Carla Bischoff, Daryl Fry, Mark and Bonnie Woods, Scott and Cassie Howard, Todd and Rachel Humphrey, Walt Carter, Mike Walters, Dennis and Linda Johnson, Brent and Margaret Yorgason, Don and Susie Campagna, Mary Ellen Hanks, Brad Wilcox, President and Sister Douglas, George Pace, Gilbert Estrada, Derick and Ruth Nordstrom, Mel and Pam White, Peter Jeppson, Tiffany and Matt Judd, Emily Hill, Envoy, Mike Stephenson, Marty Judd, Kim and Woody Cantergiani, Fred Wickling, and countless friends and relatives too numerous to mention here.

This work would have especially been improbable if not for the continued love, support, and assistance of my family—father, mother, brothers, sisters, extended family—all played enormous roles in the evolving miracles of my life. I owe all I have and am to my wonderful wife, Dallas, who has been my best friend for many years. She believes in me—what more can I say.

Finally, I wish to express appreciation to Darla Hanks Isackson, editor of Covenant Communications, Inc., and her sister, Arlene Bascom, for their professionalism, insights, and effort in bringing this work to its fruition. Without their talents and vision this book would still be only a dream.

Table of Contents

Introduction

This book is about miracles. It is about the "works of God being made manifest" in our daily lives. It's not about stupendous or earth-shattering events, but about the small private moments where the Lord reveals his mighty arm. Miracles are simply those things which, without the direct intervention of the power and priesthood of God, we could not perform by our own strength or resources.

Elder Boyd K. Packer has stated, "Some people think a miracle is only a miracle if it happens instantaneously, but miracles can grow slowly and patience and faith can compel things to happen that otherwise never would have come to pass." In the equation of priesthood, miracles, and infinite power, some of us have forgotten the critical and often essential ingredient called time. Time, which we sometimes call our enemy, miracles paradoxically embrace as friend.

This is not just a story of tragedy, love, struggle, and triumph. It is a message of hope, faith, power and miracles. It is my solemn testimony that there are, as Spencer W. Kimball declared, "infinitely more miracles today than in any age past and just as wondrous." Perhaps, with the help and influence of the Spirit, you and I may have "new eyes to see and new hearts to understand."

> "Therefore, dearly beloved brethren, let us cheerfully do all things that lie in our power; and then may we stand still, with the utmost assurance, to see the salvation of God, and for his arm to be revealed."
> (D&C 123:17.)

1

I know not why His hand is laid
In chastening on my life,
Nor why it is my little world
Is filled so full of strife;
I know not why when faith looks up
And seeks for rest from pain,
That o'er my sky fresh clouds arise
And drench my path with rain.

I know not why my prayer so long
By Him has been denied;
Nor why, while other's ships sail on,
Mine should in port abide.
But I do know that God is love,
That He my burden shares,
And though I may not understand
I know for me He cares.

I know the heights for which I long
Are often reached through pain,
I know the sheaves must needs be threshed
To yield the golden grain.
'Tis that I thus may learn to love
And know as I am known,
I will not care how rough the road
That leads me to my home.

—Grace Troy —

Chapter One
Broken Dreams

For most others in California, this Christmas, 1983, was to be like any other. The nights were crisp and cool, and the dark skies were filled with the brilliance and glow of the stars. They were nights made for romance and love. It seemed as though the stars were made just for me. This Christmas was special. It wasn't so much the day as it was the time of year for me. I had a lot of things to think about.

I had been home from my mission for one year. I was filled with the success experiences returning missionaries like to tell about. The Lord had been good to me. I felt very blessed. I also felt I was doing my part, doing the things I knew would make my Father in Heaven pleased with me. The Church and gospel were the very center of my life. I enjoyed visits to the temple, moments of solemn, heart-felt prayer, and daily feasts from the scriptures. I felt a longing to draw nearer to my God, and was acting on it.

Sports filled another vast arena in my days. Before work, after work, on the weekends, I was running off to play basketball, tennis, or ping-pong. I also enjoyed competitive waterskiing, snowskiing, bowling, golf and racquetball. It brought a surge of energy and enthusiasm for living to feel my muscles stretch, contract, and work in unison.

I was as happy as I could ever remember. My future had

never looked brighter nor more promising. It was so easy to close each day with honest praise to the giver of all good things.

The Lord had also blessed me with a wonderful girl in my life. Her name was Dallas. Unusual name for someone, I thought, but it seemed to fit the unique twinkle in her eyes. As different as her name was, however, our relationship became even more unique. We had known and dated each other for several years before my mission, having met when I was just sixteen years old.

After returning from my mission, our friendship grew into love and we became inseparable. With a romance that was built solidly on friendship, I asked her to marry me. What a happy time for both of us! The reality of our upcoming marriage left us almost breathless, as we both looked forward to spending our lives and eternities together.

The next few weeks and months were filled with plans for our wedding. We picked out colors, foods, a reception hall, and tuxedos. The list of decisions seemed endless. Before long, however, we knew it would all become happy memories and so the work became our joy.

There was just one thing that complicated matters. I lived in California, and she lived in Utah. During the years we had known and dated one another, we had to travel back and forth in order to visit. The drives were long and arduous, but worth the fun and thrill of being together.

The distance didn't make the wedding plans easier. With long conversations on the phone, sometimes until the translucent hours of the early morning, it seemed as though half the money I was making at the time was going to "Ma Bell." However, we worked through it, becoming more and more anxious to finally be together without the barrier of distance. Christmas was here, and we'd be married in just five short weeks. Or so I thought.

Christmas day was full of the usual things—music, candy, presents, and wrapping paper strewn all over the place. It felt strange, yet exhilarating, to receive gifts that related directly to our upcoming marriage and were meant to be used by the two of us. The gifts made me think of my sweetheart, because, as usual, we were apart again, trying to enjoy Christmas with our families. But, we'd be together soon! Immediately after dinner I would be packing my little car and driving off through the night to be with her, to enjoy at least part of the Christmas holidays together.

Little did I know how much my life would change after that night. Everything I believed in and held dear would be challenged and tested. Was I ready? Why didn't I even suspect? My world, as I then knew it, was about to crumble all around me. I was standing at the gateway to experiences I would not have wished on my worst enemy.

Leaving for Utah that Christmas night seemed no different than all the times I had gone before. I had made the trip dozens of times through the years with friends and family. It was no big deal. We had a family prayer before I left, as we always did. Kneeling in a formation which never quite resembled a "family circle," we prayed for the usual things you would pray for before such a trip: a safe journey, the Spirit to guide my actions, and that God would keep and protect me until I arrived. No one even thought that maybe things would be different this time.

I was traveling with a new friend of mine, named John. We drove away at about 8 o'clock that Christmas evening. It was dark and cool outside. As I slowly inhaled the fresh country air, I felt my body come alive with the exhilaration of the trip and the anticipation of being with Dallas again.

The roads were dry, and we had decided to drive the southern route through Nevada and Las Vegas in order to avoid any possibility of snow over the northern mountain pass in California. I was excited to finally be on my way. In fifteen short hours I'd be with my future bride, my best friend, and we'd be sharing affection and Christmas gifts.

I drove for the first eight hours of the trip, mostly through California and into Nevada. By then my eyes felt heavy and it was John's turn at the wheel. He had been resting for some time now, and I was ready for some sleep. I comfortably arranged myself in the reclined passenger seat, fastened my seat belt, and quickly dozed off as John drove on into the night.

What seemed only minutes later (but was actually more than an hour and a half) I was suddenly awakened as I felt the car swerve. John had fallen asleep at the wheel, lost control of the car, and it was heading for a cement barrier along the right side of the highway. "Hold on!" John yelled, and I heard the frightened desperation in his voice.

Trying to avoid the wall, he pulled hard to the left. But it was too late. The car, traveling at freeway speed, hit the cement embankment. The tires rode the embankment to the top, hurtling the car over it. The car, a little Volkswagen Rabbit, rolled down the side of the road, each rotation strewing pieces of metal and glass along the way, until it came to a stop in an unrecognizable form. John later told me what happened then. With his white-knuckled hands still clinging to the steering wheel, he immediately looked to see if I was all right. His heart stopped: I was gone!

John quickly pulled himself from the tangled mass of metal

6

into a world thick with new fears. His blood ran cold with eerie feelings he could only later refer to as approaching death.

His voice rang out in the clear night, "Art! Art!" Listening intently, only the quiet sounds of a gentle wind whispered back. Fear washed over him in a wave of terror. "Art!" he yelled again, now running blindly in the darkness and stumbling on the rough terrain. No answer. Finally, on hands and knees, John groped through the thick darkness, feeling his way, calling my name again and again. After what seemed an eternity in a dark world, he heard soft groans of pain and rushed to my side. It was 4 o'clock in the morning; still dark and very cold.

When I regained consciousness, I was lying on the floor of the Nevada desert without much idea of what was happening. But I knew I wasn't dead yet, because I was hurting too much.

My face was badly scraped and bloody, and my lips were torn and swollen. Fortunately, I did not know then what had really happened. I had done the unthinkable; I had broken my neck and now I was passing in and out between reality and unconsciousness. I had always thought that when a person broke his neck, he died. It was that simple in my mind. All I knew was that something was seriously wrong.

When I seemed somewhat coherent, John asked me how I was doing. I told him things were not right—I could not feel my legs. I asked him if he would give me a priesthood blessing and promise me that my legs would be all right and that I'd recover. He said he didn't know if he could do that. I pleaded with him to ask the Lord if he could. Humbly, anxiously, John knelt beside his hurting friend and petitioned God to open the windows of heaven and bless his frightened children.

The air seemed still and calm as two priesthood bearers approached their Lord in prayer. A dark, cold desert became a temple where God and men became peacefully close. With the power of great rushing winds, yet with the whisper of a still, small voice, God gave his approval for such a blessing. John, now with deep confidence, laid his hands upon my head and pronounced the blessing in the healing name of Jesus Christ. He blessed me that I would walk again—that I would recover completely and be healed. That was all I needed to hear. The salt from my tears stung my wounded face, and I sank back into unconsciousness.

Minutes following the accident, truck drivers saw us and radioed for emergency help. Because the accident occurred some forty miles east of Las Vegas, it was nearly an hour before an ambulance could arrive on the scene. In the meantime, John took his leather jacket off and placed it across my broken body to keep me warm until help arrived.

I remember part of the forty-five minute ambulance ride to the Las Vegas Community Hospital. A great battle was taking place inside me. It seemed I could feel my spirit slipping away. John and the ambulance attendant tried to keep me awake, aware that I was in danger of shutting my eyes for the last time in this life. "What day is it?" they asked. I didn't know. "What day was yesterday? It was a special day, a holiday, do you remember?" they inquired.

I searched my mind, I didn't know. They asked again, "How many lights do you see on the ceiling?"

I responded, "Four." They were making progress.

"Who were you going to see in Utah?" was the last question I remember them asking.

"My sweetheart—the most beautiful girl in the world." Knowing the pain of my circumstances, the attendant looked with skepticism and then surprise, at the smile which softened my mouth as I slipped into unconsciousness again.

My eyes opened slowly and painfully as I looked up into the bright lights of the emergency room. A doctor was standing over me stitching my forehead, lips and nose. It was hard for me to see. I later learned that one of my eyes was filled with blood and was swollen beyond recognition. I heard muffled voices, none that I could distinguish. A prayer left my lips, "God, please help me," and I was gone again.

Reflections by Dallas

December 26th: I awoke to the humming of my alarm clock and immediately remembered that today was special. Yesterday was special also, it was Christmas. Today was Monday and I would normally be taking advantage of the chance to sleep in, but I had much to do. It was 7:00 now and by noon Art would be driving up my street, into my driveway and finally he'd walk through the front door and into my arms. I had it all pictured so well in my mind. It had happened that way so many times before and I felt a growing excitement.

I quickly made my bed and headed into my parents' bedroom. Mom and Dad were having their morning prayer, kneeling side by side next to their bed. I smiled as I tip-toed back down the hall. I loved to see my parents praying together. They would usually pray with their door open, but it wasn't until a few years ago that I figured out why: they wanted to set an example, and have their children learn from it.

Art would be staying in my brother Scott's room so I went downstairs to freshen it up and to put clean linens on the bed. I also had a special Christmas card that I tucked away under the covers for Art to find that night. We enjoyed leaving little notes around to surprise each other.

For the next hour or so I helped put the remnants of Christmas away. There were boxes of paper and bows everywhere, and still lying under the tree were two wrapped packages. Art and I would open our gifts to each other that night by the fire. I was so glad he was coming out to spend some of the holidays with me. We had a wonderful day planned and I had already called a friend to confirm the time we'd go snowmobiling later that afternoon. Art had never been snowmobiling and was especially excited.

Despite the fact that it was winter, the day seemed bright and cheerful to me. Perfect weather to be outdoors, I thought. I was glad it was good driving weather for Art, also. "Dear Father in Heaven," I prayed silently as I did my laundry, "I'm thankful for the good weather today and pray that Art and John will continue to drive safely—that they will be protected in all they do. I feel so blessed to have such a wonderful man in my life and that we can be sealed in thy temple."

My little prayer was interrupted by the ringing of the phone and I playfully looked upward and said, "Hold that thought!" My arms were full of clothes as I raced to the phone. Hugging the phone with my shoulder, I answered brightly, reflecting my happy mood. A familiar voice was on the other line; it was Art's mother, Betty.

I could feel the forced control in her voice as she asked, "Dallas, are you sitting down?"

My heart skipped a beat at the question. No one asks if you're sitting down unless there is something wrong. I sat down and waited fearfully for what she had to say. She paused and then told me news that made my heart race. "Art and John were involved in a serious car accident this morning. I just got off the phone with John and they're in Las Vegas."

I felt panic but I talked to myself saying, "Okay, so he's been in an accident but he'll be fine. He's had dozens of close calls before, but he's always all right." Betty continued, "John is okay but Art—he's been hurt, badly. John fell asleep at the wheel and the car hit a cement abutment and rolled. Art was thrown from the car and has a broken neck." The clothes fell from my arms.

I immediately felt sick and completely numb. No, this could not be! It had to be an awful trick, and any second Art would come leaping through the front door with a big smile. Nothing bad could happen to Art. Especially not anything as serious as a broken neck.

As Art grew up he had had many brushes with disaster and serious injury, and had always emerged unharmed. As a nine year old, Art had tried to parachute from the roof of their two story home by grasping the four corners of a bedsheet and jumping. About the time he passed the balcony, he realized he wasn't going to slow down! Aside from walking a little belabored for an afternoon, all that came from the experience were a few good laughs for years to come. Art's spirit of adventure drove him past the edge of safety time after time, whether in sports, motorcycle riding, driving a car, or just horsing around. Less than a year earlier, while driving home from Utah to California, his car hit "black ice" on the freeway and the car slid out of control off the road. Once the tires of the car met the sloping shoulder, the car flipped onto its side and continue to slide for another hundred feet or more. When the car finally came to a stop, it fell back onto all four wheels! Art and his brother, Paul, just laughed! They were used to near-misses. Art's myriad of experiences where he should have been left badly injured, but wasn't, gave everyone, including Art, the feeling that he was invincible—nothing could hurt Art.

This time, we were wrong.

I immediately had thoughts of Jill Kinmont and the movie about her I'd seen on television. Terrible things happened to her and she was in a wheelchair. There was no way Art would be in a wheelchair. We were going to be married in five short weeks . . . my mind trailed off as I heard Betty say, "It appears that Art is paralyzed from the chest down, but they're really not sure how serious it is. He's in intensive care." With all the control I had mustered now seeping out of me, tears began to roll down my cheeks. I could hardly see through my tears as I wrote down the name of the hospital and Art's room number.

As I hung up the receiver, I began to sob uncontrollably. I made my way into my parents bedroom where Mom was cutting Dad's hair. They both looked at me, startled by my sobbing as I sank to the floor and buried my face in my hands. Rushing over to me, they finally understood enough of my muddled words to know what was happening. Then with the two of them on the floor beside me and their arms of love encircling me, we cried. We cried for Art, and we cried for me. We cried for all those who knew and loved him. From my conversation with Betty, I didn't know if he would still be alive by the time any of us reached him. We prayed that God would spare his life and watch over his struggling body.

If a heart could truly break, I knew that mine had broken that day. My whole body ached as our years of memories flooded my mind. We had spent so much time together developing our friendship and our relationship. Art was all I had ever wanted and the weight of the possibility of never seeing him again was almost too much to bear. I was used to feeling in control and having confidence, or at least the ability to fake it, when going into almost any situation. I felt so helpless now. It was as though the walls of my life were caving in on me with no way to escape or to hide. Closing my eyes wasn't going to make it go away. This was life as real as I'd ever imagined it.

I didn't want my world to change or my plans to be altered. Change is scary. I wondered if I would recognize Art or if he would recognize me. Could I bear to see him hurting? What would he look like and would this tragic, life-altering experience change his heart; change the person I had grown to love with all my heart? It was easy to imagine his being bitter; I had seen others become hard and calloused by such trials. Not that I could ever imagine those qualities in Art, but the nature of the experience seemed almost too powerful, even for him.

With all these thoughts crowding my mind, my main thought was still how quickly I could leave. Because of the holidays, the phone lines to the airport were busy but we finally got through. I packed, not knowing how long I'd be away or where I'd stay and my parents drove me to the Salt Lake airport to catch a flight to Las Vegas to be with Art.

As we entered the huge marble corridors, I stopped in my tracks. Standing alone a few feet from me was a silver and gray wheelchair. Two weeks ago my brother, Michael, and I had been at this airport looking at that same chair. At the time, I had plopped myself down in it and Michael had pushed me around trying to keep occupied while waiting for a friend's flight that had been delayed. Feeling adventuresome, I pretended to be crippled and in need of that chair. I remember the looks of curiosity and pity I received. But I was ready with an answer to their questioning eyes—I had been in an accident. When we left the airport, I was able to bound out of that chair at my own command and go on with my life.

That fun night's memories melted into fear as I looked at the wheelchair now. What had once been a toy to me could become

13

an intimate part of Art's life, and unlike me, he wouldn't be able to just walk away. Not even wanting to be near that chair now, I slowly moved away, found my gate, and said a tearful goodbye to my parents as I boarded the plane to Las Vegas.

It seemed an eternity before I reached the hospital and my sweetheart. As the plane lifted into the sky, my mind raced so fast I could hardly stand it. I didn't want to think about what lay ahead. I wanted to think about Art with his warm voice telling me "Merry Christmas!" over the phone just the evening before, expressing feelings of love and thoughts of being together. He had tried to pry information out of me about my wedding dress and what it looked like. It was such a happy conversation and feelings were so strong. And then I remembered the last words I spoke, "Be careful, Art. I need you."

But now, to know that Art wasn't okay, that my plane might not even fly fast enough to reach him before he died, was almost more than I could bear. I called the hospital but no one seemed to know his condition. Or was it that they wouldn't tell, trying to protect me? Either way, not knowing was maddening. I was terribly frightened, for both of us.

Leaving the cab, which had taken me from the airport to the hospital, I found myself trembling as the automatic doors of the emergency room flew open and I approached the front desk. This was all too real—the smells, the noises, the pain. With an uncertain voice, I asked which floor Art was on and headed in that direction. On one hand I wanted to run to Art as fast as I could, and yet on the other I wanted to stall, as if that would change things. The elevator jerked to a stop, and with a prayer on my lips, I stepped out.

Down the hall I could see John's familiar face. He was standing slumped against the wall. He had blood on his white pants and orange polo shirt. His arm was in a sling and he was crying softly. He hadn't seen me yet, and so I gently touched his arm. His head jerked up, and there was incredible hurt in his eyes. I felt an immediate sense of love and compassion for this friend whose heart had broken also. "Is he alive?" I asked.

"Yes, but they say he'll never walk again." John spoke these words so softly I could hardly hear him. I hugged John, then walked slowly to Art's room and opened the door. Seeing him for the first time took my breath away. His body lay so still and silent as my eyes traveled up to his face. It was a tangle of tubes and hoses, scrapes and blood. The worst thing for me was seeing the huge metal tongs imbedded in the sides of his head where thirty pounds of weight hung from a traction bar. This I hadn't expected and it made my knees weak. I stood there for a moment and then took Art's hand in mine. He slowly opened his eyes and it was as though someone had opened the curtains and let light pour into the room. Suddenly, all the questions I had harbored seemed so petty, irrelevant and naive. I knew in an instant that Art would be all right. When I looked into his tired, swollen eyes, I saw more than just pain, I saw an indomitable will to survive. Even more than that, I saw a determination to triumph. He took the fear from my heart and replaced it with strength and love.

He whispered "Hello," and I, who had come to comfort him, found that I was the one being comforted. I became the recipient of peace. I came to bring him assurances, yet he assured me. I came with a whisper of hope, and he promised me the world. In answer to my earlier questioning mind, he recognized me instantly. I also knew he was the same man I'd fallen in love with. We fell in love again in those first moments. We smiled, and faced a new, uncertain future, together. Even in the midst of more sadness than I could imagine, would come happiness greater than I'd ever known.

When trouble comes your soul to try,
You love the friend who just "stands by."
Perhaps there is nothing he can do—
The thing is strictly up to you;
For there are troubles all your own,
And paths the soul must tread alone;
Times when love can't smooth the road
Nor friendship lift the heavy load,
But just to know you have a friend
Who will "stand by" until the end,
Whose sympathy, through all endures,
Whose warm handclasp is always yours—
And so with fervent heart you cry,
"God bless the friend who just 'stands by'."

(Author Unknown)

Chapter Two
No Man is an Island

When I awoke again I felt different and awkward. Although heavily drugged, I could still feel the sharp sting of pain. I had undergone four hours of surgery to mend my broken neck. It had been broken at the fifth vertebrae—a little higher and I would have most assuredly been dead. They had made an incision about three inches long on the front of my neck to fuse the three vertebrae together. A tube was connected to the back of my neck to help drain off the excess blood.

I could feel tubes in my nose that went to my stomach, in an effort to keep me nourished, since I could not eat on my own. Worst of all, however, were the cold, metal tongs that had been bolted into the sides of my head, with thirty pounds of weight attached, to keep the pressure off the wounded area. My moustache was still filled with dried blood and the sides of my head had been shaved to provide a clean surface for the tongs to be inserted. I looked a mess. My mouth felt like cotton and it was hard to swallow. My body felt as though it weighed a hundred tons. No degree of effort would move it, and I was trapped inside.

The first person, other than John, I could recognize beside my bed was my beautiful fiancé, Dallas. Until that moment, I felt I had endured an eternity of pain and instability, but a great strength came as I saw her face. She meant more to me than anything, and seeing her meant I was safe again. What I was experiencing was some ugly nightmare that merely needed great light to dispel it.

She did bring light, but the nightmare persisted. Dallas was my sweetheart, the girl of all my boyhood dreams. When we were together, we laughed and played, we shared and dreamed. She made me feel important, like a king. She had told me that to love me was the greatest joy of her life. My heart ached.

My first thoughts when I saw her by my bed were to protect her. I knew her heart was literally breaking as she stood bravely beside me. I was suffering, but none of that seemed important anymore. How could I bring light and joy back into her life and take her away from all the awful smells and sights of pain?

Through the personal struggles of my mission I had learned the benefits of optimism. A great mission president had given me a new set of glasses to wear, through which I had learned to see the world differently. I put those glasses on again now. I knew at this time I could not give Dallas much, but at least I would try to lend her strength, peace, and hope.

"Hello, Sweetheart," were the only words I could muster before tears began to cloud my vision. I struggled to push my emotions back. I could not and would not allow fear to be seen. I had to overcome the pain, even for a moment, to lend courage where courage was needed.

Looking back now, I don't think I needed to fight my feelings and emotions so hard. As I would learn later, during the weeks and months spent in the hospitals and in therapy sessions, Dallas would prove to be a great strength. I should have known that. Her source of strength came from the same living fountain as mine.

For now, I needed her so much. Although her coming

confirmed the reality of my nightmare, still, hers was the face I had most anxiously awaited. Seeing her, peace had found its place once again in my heart, and as I began drifting off to sleep my mind raced back over the years of our relationship.

I met Dallas when I was sixteen years old while on a vacation with my family in Utah. Over the years we had written, called, and visited each other. The early infatuation was the beginning of a beautiful, lasting relationship that would eventually blossom into marriage. However, I never suspected the stony paths we would be required to travel together before that dream would become a reality.

In those youthful years I had learned to dream. I dreamed about romance, adventure, success, prosperity, and happiness. I dreamed of beautiful sunsets, white horses, and living "happily ever after." Nowhere in those dreams was there place for tragedy, suffering, or pain. Neither had I learned that growth and great miracles can come from experiences interlaced with struggle. While I dreamed of blue skies and green, smooth paths, I thought pain, suffering, and tragedy were reserved for the "other guy." I had no idea that it was to be *through* the pain and suffering that the greatest blessings and miracles of my own life would come. I would not be left alone to shed the tears of a lonely traveler, but rather, through the miracle of time and circumstance, I would be given opportunities which would bring blessings untold. The dreams of my younger years would come to fruition, but only as I became the "other guy."

The room was dark and quiet. The movement of new people in and out had decreased as only a few (including Dallas) remained behind to hope, pray, and tend to my needs. The doctors had done what they could. Only time would tell what my future would be. For now, it seemed as though time was all I had. I did not yet fully understand how significant the role of time would become and the miracles that would result because of it.

Silently, my door opened, spilling the light from the corridor into my room and letting in the noise from the busy nurses down the hall. I couldn't see who walked in, since my eyes were fixed on the ceiling because of the hideous-looking "ice-clamp" attached to my head, but I could sense them. It was Dallas's mother and father who had come from Utah. With them came even more strength and assurance. They came and stood beside my bed. Mom's eyes were moist with tears and showed deep hurt. I knew she was suffering with me. Dad stood beside her, always a source of strength and courage. Yet, he was obviously touched emotionally and showed signs of anguish and pain for me. I have no doubt that, if possible, they would have taken my place rather than watch me suffer. My love grew for those two special people a hundred fold as our hearts meshed together in that moment of time.

I broke the silence, "Hi, Mom. Isn't this great? Please just pray for me . . . that I learn the things I need to learn." Maybe that sounds a little trite to you, but it came from the depths of my heart. From the moment priesthood hands, endowed with power from on high, were laid upon my head, I knew this experience would bring good things into my life. While I hurt physically until my whole being seemed to beg for relief, my spirit praised the God that made and loved me. Somehow, I knew these things would "be for my good." Not eventually, but today, as well as in my forevers.

It hurt to see other people hurting for me. Many would eventually come to offer assurance, hope, love and comfort. Each knew, to some degree, the type of mental, spiritual and physical anguish I was suffering. When they came to me in the hospital, I could see the depth of pain in their eyes and hear it in their voices.

What tore me up inside more than anything, except the suffering of my beautiful fiancé, was the anguish of my own parents. When my mom and dad walked into my dark and gloomy hospital room that first day in Las Vegas, my emotions flowed. I was completely overwhelmed. All the emotional control I had reserved for my precious fiancé and other family and friends was exhausted, and I cried like a baby for the first time.

Their hearts were broken, and I felt powerless to mend them. Here was their son, whose life had been largely free of physical discomfort and pain, being given a harsh and cold lesson in adversity.

I looked first at my father and said, "I'm sorry we wrecked your car. I'll get you a new one, I promise." I saw emotions rise to the surface in a man who was rarely emotional.

Holding his shaky composure he replied, "That's okay, Son. You'll be all right," and he placed his big hand gently on my bruised shoulder.

You will never know the impact those words had on me. They still ring in my ears today whenever things get hard: "Son, you'll be all right." You see, my dad has always been a powerful man, physically, spiritually, and in his career. He was never one for many words, but his words always seemed to carry an impact. What Dad said was always true, and in my heart I knew I'd be all right as soon as he said it.

My mother's pain was written plainly across her beautiful face. She stood beside my father, leaving me assurances that she would be right there as long as I needed her. Indeed, my needs were great. The next ten days were more horrifying and distressful than I could have imagined. Vivid in my memory are the countless hours my mother spent by my bedside, so many hours that it seemed she was there days on end. She had seen pain and suffering before in her children's lives.

She herself was acquainted with pain, having given birth to seven children, although my injuries and anguish were more than she had ever witnessed. She offered unmeasured strength during some of my weakest hours. There were others who shared that post with her around the clock, but in my mind she was a guardian angel whose love for me was deeper than I had previously known, and whose presence brought unmeasured strength and courage.

As the challenge of my accident presented a physical struggle, it also presented a powerful spiritual and mental fight, even from the beginning. During my days in Las Vegas a constant battle seemed to be taking place. On one side was all the good, right, and encouraging things in my life led by the Lord himself. On the opposing side was Satan and his hosts, complete with all of the negative and degrading things the evil one would have me feel. In those first few days I came to understand and appreciate the vast difference in roles between these two opposing forces and the length and depth to which they would go to hurt me or to rescue me.

The first four nights, after a long surgery, were sleepless ones for me. It certainly wasn't that I didn't want to sleep. My body was exhausted from the trauma of the accident. However, as night would fall and I would try to sleep I began to hear voices in my mind. I heard laughter; it was a hideous sound. For a long time these voices and laughter were unrecognizable. All I knew was that the source must somehow be evil because of the fear it created in me. I fought sleep, terrified of the things I was hearing and feeling.

After a time the voices became more distinguishable. A hauntingly familiar voice now began to ring clear. Satan's voice resounded, "I've got you now. I have destroyed your life.

Without your body you are nothing. You'll live a despicable life, and when it is over, I will have won." I heard it over and over again. And then there was the laughter; it seemed to come from hundreds of voices.

For four days I feared the nights. I asked my family and John to stay and sit with me, believing they could protect me from these feelings. I found that as long as someone I loved was touching me, even though I could not always feel the touch because of the paralysis, I could rest and sleep peacefully. However, no matter how deep the sleep or how light the touch, as soon as a loved hand was lifted from my body I awoke immediately with fear in my eyes and voice. As I slowly understood the source of my fear, my family and I turned to the only power that could help us. In prayer, and through the power of the priesthood, we asked God to send his ministering angels to guard the way. Peace returned to our little room from that moment on, and I was free. Fear was destroyed, and faith, assurance, and hope were ushered in to be my constant companions.

In a unique and powerful way, I learned how Satan uses difficult crossroads in our lives to attempt to destroy us by tempting us to be bitter, angry, or discouraged. However, in contrast, with the added strength of the priesthood and of people who love us, we render the evil one powerless in our lives. It became clear to me that Satan has no voice, except we give him one. He has no will, except we make his ours. He has no power, unless we forfeit our free agency—the control of our minds and hearts—to him.

How do we render the evil one powerless in our own personal lives? Even the blackest, thickest darkness must begin to dispel at the first glimpses of spiritual light. By turning our thoughts to the Lord, adding light upon light, the darkness will

23

flee to the farthest corners of the universe. The Lord has orchestrated a marvelous plan whereby darkness cannot overcome light. However, light can always destroy darkness. I desire light. Light is truth; light is the love of Christ; light is forever.

How can a young man put a price on that knowledge of being loved by the Lord and his family? How do you place a value on seeing your father cry for the first time because he loves you? How do you put into perspective the powerful influence of a nurturing mother over her hurting son? As I grew up I always knew that I was loved. It was spoken and shown. However, under the weight of difficult circumstances, our hearts and feelings united in a unique and powerful way. Emotions were felt and expressed in such a way that bonded them to our hearts forever. The effects of this bonding became a significant and meaningful miracle in my struggling life.

While many suffer heartache, tragedy, illness, and other painful experiences throughout life, no one suffers alone. Family members and friends often feel the sting of pain and the burden of heartache as deeply as human hearts can reach.

The Lord also suffers with us as he has promised that we will be "supported . . . against all the fiery darts of the adversary . . ." and that he will be with us "in every time of trouble." (D&C 3:8.)

Tragedy and struggle have a way of reaching out and affecting others. Each person plays a vital role in coping with, overcoming, enduring, and participating in the wonder of the miracles which come.

When in the dim beginning of the years,
God mixed in man the raptures and the tears,
And scattered through his brain that starry stuff,
He said: "Behold! Yet this is not enough;
For I must test his spirit to make sure
That he can dare the vision and endure.

I will withdraw my face,
Veil me in shadow for a certain space,
Leaving behind me only a broken clue–
A crevice where the glory glimmers through,
Some whisper from the sky,
Some footprint in the road to track me by.

I will leave man to make the fateful guess,
To leave him torn between the no and yes,
Leave him unresting 'til he rest in me,
Drawn upward by the choice that makes him free–
Leave him in tragic loneliness to choose,
With all in life to win or to lose."

—Edwin Markam—

Chapter Three
The Testing—Why?

Las Vegas, the city of lights, a city that never sleeps, still reminds me of some of my most terrifying, as well as meaningful, experiences. Las Vegas Valley Medical was the small community hospital where I was taken following the accident. The first ten days of my new life began there, not under the most favorable of circumstances.

When I was wheeled through those swinging emergency room doors, I was greeted by a staff of nurses who were confused and inexperienced when it came to someone suffering from such extensive injuries. Unfortunately, they caused me some additional suffering. They did their best to help relieve my pain, but lack of experience and knowledge can overshadow even the sincerest of desires.

Those first ten days of my life in the hospital were more miserable than I could have ever conceived. In a very real sense, it was a living hell.

In order for us to understand, to find some purpose in pain and struggle, we must travel back to our pre-existent state when you and I, and all of our Father in Heaven's children sat together in a great and grand council in heaven. A plan was presented—a perfect plan. The Lord told us we would be sent here to earth to obtain physical bodies. But, the message that we would be given the opportunity to become like him thrilled us the most. The scriptures say that we "shouted for joy." But then, I believe, he told us something else. He said, "It's going to be hard, but I will be with you. You don't have to be alone." Then, with the sealing power of his word, covenants were entered into and promises made which were meant to lift our hearts so we could endure the struggle and pains of a lifetime.

Once on earth, however, many are tempted to "curse God and die," as Job's friends pleaded for him to do. But, Job sensed a greater purpose in his sufferings, one that he had yet to understand. I, too, have many things I still don't understand, but my experiences have provided more than sufficient understanding for now, and have left me with deep feelings of love for him who "descended below them all."

While many friends made their way to my bedside, others wrote letters, sent flowers, made phone calls, fasted, and prayed. As I lay there in my bed, struggling for peace and reassurance, my mother read to me from the piles of letters that had been sent. Tears rolled down my face as I listened to the words of people who cared, even though many of them didn't even know me.

I turned my eyes upward again, and in my heart I cried out to the Lord. It all seemed so unfair, so unjust. I had reached a point where I had to get answers to some questions that were inside me. The words of my mission president, "The eleventh commandment is, 'Thou shalt not think that life is fair,'" echoed in my mind. Still, I needed answers.

Shutting myself into the world of my heart and mind, I plead, "Can you hear their voices, Lord? Do you hear the many cries and pleas in my behalf? I'm hurting, Lord. I'm hurting really bad. Do you know that? Do you know where I am? Do you know who I am? Can you . . . will you help me?"

At the time of my prayer, my mother-in-law had been

massaging my foot. Of course, I could not feel her touch. Suddenly, I had feeling in my foot for the first time since the accident! Oh, it was not as you would feel yours now, but nevertheless, I could feel it. For anyone who has ever sustained a serious spinal cord injury, this is the first, significant offering of hope. In my enthusiasm, I shared this new-found knowledge with those who were with me. We laughed and we cried. Those new physical feelings have never left, but have persisted even to this day, and have even spread through most other parts of my body.

Then another, very different, feeling came. I felt a presence I had not felt before. Into my mind and heart came some reassuring and powerful words I will never forget. A voice said, "Remember, Art, back a long, long time ago, when you and I sat in a great council in heaven. Remember, I said you could become like me. You thrilled at the idea. But, then I told you it would be hard, sometimes very hard. I promised you, however, with an oath and a covenant, that I would never leave you to suffer alone. Art, when you suffer, I suffer. When you hurt, I hurt. And, when you cry, I cry. I promised you then, and I will not leave you now."

Echoing down through the corridor of years since the accident, the power of those words still rings clearly their message of truth. The Lord told the Prophet Joseph Smith, "What I say unto one I say unto all, be of good cheer, little children; for I am in your midst, and I have not forsaken you." (D&C 61:36.)

What joy came into my heart! An enormous burden had been lifted. A dark and pain-filled room now was illuminated with glorious rays of light and truth. God had spoken, and in his speaking, he brought me a peace I had never felt before. Tears flowed freely. I looked at my mother's beautiful face, smiled, closed my eyes, and slept like a baby, for the first time in four days.

Those were the beginnings for me of some of the greatest blessings I have received in my life. I know that sounds like somewhat of a paradox, but it is true. As I recall the words I heard in my mind and heart that night, I am led to say, "I thank God that life is hard." Because he loves us, he does not stop the unfolding of natural law, and he allows us to be hurt. Somehow, through all the tears and all the inexpressible joy, we can work to become like him. I thrill at the thought. Even today, I shout for joy. I thank God that life is hard.

As my mind reflects back over a young lifetime of emotional and physical bumps and bruises, I relate those things to the feelings I was given in the hospital that day. While we enjoy the sweet fruit of life, we also have many experiences with the bitter. However, in the context of our purpose and promises, I am led to repeat, "I thank God that life is hard."

Hasn't life always been hard for everybody, regardless of age or position? I remember when I was just a little boy. My mother had made me the most wonderful thing in the whole world—a little blue blanket. I looked just like Linus as I dragged that blanket with me everywhere I went. I slept with it, took it to church with me, ate with it by my side, and played with it. Then, one night, I searched everywhere for that little blue blanket, but my efforts were to no avail; I couldn't find it. My mother said it was lost and I'd have to go to bed without it. I cried myself to sleep that night and remember thinking then that life was hard.

On a warm summer evening, when I was fourteen, I went with my brother and some friends to see a movie. My mother drove us to the theatre and told us where to meet her when it was time to be picked up. As we waited for my mother in the dark parking lot in front of the mall, some men, better than twice my age, thought it would be fun to beat up on some young kids. I helped my friends to escape, but was caught by the men. They left me hurt, bleeding, and scared. I remember thinking then that life was hard, but now I was learning from it.

The words which came to me as I struggled in the hospital, and the lessons I was learning, brought to my mind the thoughts, feelings, and words of a prayer I had spoken not too long before. Only three weeks before my accident, I had attended a fireside where Peter Jeppson was the speaker. I had listened intently as he described the horror of having his body completely burned in an automobile accident. Tears fell from my eyes as he portrayed pain and suffering beyond my understanding. After years of struggle, operations, and enduring, he emphatically spoke of the strength and testimony which had come into his life. He revealed the sweet experiences that had joined his heart and spirit more intimately with the Savior. And then he shared the most profound truth I had heard him speak, "I am who am I today, *because* of my experience." What an impact that statement had on me!

I went home that night a new person. I quietly reflected on every word he had shared. As I lay there in my bed, my pillow became wet with my tears. Softly, I slipped from the warmth of my bed and onto my knees. "Dear Father," I prayed, "while I don't desire the pain and struggles of Peter Jeppson, with all my heart I desire to become like him and like thee—to become the person I am meant to become. While I fear pain and shudder at the thought of suffering, I am more afraid of failing to live up to my divine potential. If my potential requires a suffering more intense than I can even imagine, please, regardless of my fears, don't withhold the opportunity from me.

Don't misunderstand—I wasn't asking to be hurt, or maimed, or crippled. I wasn't asking to be tested. After a lifetime of prayers which included "protect me from harm," "watch over me continually," and other "don't let me ever be

30

hurt" phrases, I was asking for the opportunity to grow, to learn, and to change. If that process required extreme pain and anguish, I did not want it withheld because of my own fears and weaknesses. For the first time in my life I began to understand the supreme role of pain in the process of learning and growth, and I did not want to be denied. If there could be an easier way to learn, I would have gladly desired it. Our experiences are individual and our needs unique. I just wanted the Lord to know I was willing. I had heard my mission president say before, "We are often desirous to eat of the Savior's loaves, but unwilling to drink of his bitter cup."

My feelings resolved, I climbed back into my bed and drifted to sleep. I never imagined how those heart-felt words would change my life forever. That night I had finally surrendered my will to the Lord's, regardless of how hard the road might be. (However, I still don't believe the Lord *causes* accidents—rather he *allows* natural law to proceed uninterrupted if it will be for our ultimate long-range good.)

On that Christmas night, and in the days and weeks to follow, every belief most sacred to my heart was challenged and put to the test. Under this new set of circumstances, my beliefs were dissected and examined, explored and investigated. I felt at times as though my heart was being wrenched. But, when the shock and trauma of a new struggle subsided, my beliefs stood firm and true.

A special doctor, one who was not on the hospital staff, was brought into the Las Vegas Medical Center to handle my needs. He was a good doctor, experienced in his field, but it seemed difficult for him to understand or involve himself emotionally in the traumatizing experiences of his patients.

In those first days and months spent in the hospitals, none of the experts seemed to want to give assurance of anything but the worst. Words were guarded and pessimism prevailed. It was hard for me, and even harder for others, to accept the gloom and negativity of those whom we thought should offer hope and encouragement. We learned quickly, in efforts to avoid the pain, to look within ourselves for sources of assurance. From the beginning, God planted in our hearts seeds of faith and hope. His assurances and promises were not always time specific, but they were consistent and persistent.

With the glorious blessing I had received there on the desert floor, and the numerous blessings given later echoing the same promises, we often felt a sense of urgency or impatience in our "waiting upon the Lord." While blessings given made promises of complete eventual recovery, they also declared that the purpose of that miracle would be to act as a witness to others of the power and extent of the Lord's priesthood. Because of my complete recovery, others would come to know of the reality of the Savior and his omnipotence. One man who gave me such a blessing, later made reference to the experience as one of the most spiritually profound moments of his life. Even with knowledge and faith, however, it was hard not to expect immediate results. We were very willing for the promised miracle to happen immediately—but what was the Lord's will?

In the beginning, our expectations ran high as we desired to put a wristwatch on God, with an alarm set for an hour of our personal convenience. As time passed, I was slowly tutored in the essence and reality of adversity, and began to learn the role time plays in the working of miracles. Consequently, my attitudes and vision changed.

Years later, as I write these words, tears come to my eyes as I consider the promises the Lord has granted me. You may wonder, however, what became of those grand and marvelous blessings. If you were here with me today, you would see me sitting before you in a wheelchair, still crippled from a devastating accident. My hands are chapped, rough and dry from years of pushing myself from place to place; my paralyzed fingers are curled and stiff from disuse. My legs are thin and wiry from sitting for so long.

Seeing me, you might ask "Why?" when one instantaneous miracle could have stemmed the suffering, pain, and anguish of years. Why, if the promise of complete recovery was declared, should I still be suffering today? Why, if the Lord's priesthood has the power and authority to heal and deliver from pain, misery, and struggle, should I be denied that blessing after years of waiting?

I don't know the full answer to these questions. I do know, however, as sure as I am alive, that when I have done all I need to do while in this wheelchair, when I have accomplished all God intends for me to accomplish in this condition, when I have learned the things I need to learn, then God *will* open the windows of heaven and pour out those blessings.

I will most assuredly walk again in some future mortal day. For some this is hard to understand; for me, it is a reality. I know the power of the priesthood is real. I know that God lives, and that he loves his children. God is not dead, nor has his priesthood lost its power. It functions today as it did in times past when our Savior walked among mortal men, and miracles have not ceased. God has spoken these truths to my heart. However, God's glorious ways are not our ways and are not always clear.

While we do not know and understand all things, there are some things we do know. Some designs *are* clear. Some truths have been revealed which bring meaning to the seemingly meaningless.

It is my solemn witness that God lives, and that Jesus is the Christ. He lives and loves us and desires our happiness always. He died for us, not because he had to, but because he wanted to. He would die again, if it would help us. Through Christ and the Father, a plan was laid out which gave purpose and promise to mortal life, even though Satan would declare it meaningless and futile.

Spencer W. Kimball once declared:

The basic gospel law is free agency. To force us to be careful or righteous would be to nullify that fundamental law, and *growth would be impossible.*

Should we be protected always from hardship, pain, suffering, or labor? Should the Lord protect the righteous? Should he immediately punish the wicked? If growth comes from fun and ease and aimless responsibility, then why should we ever exert ourselves to work or learn or overcome? If success is measured by the years we live, then death is failure and tragedy. If earth life is the ultimate, how can we justify death, even in old age? If we look at mortality as a complete existence, then pain, sorrow, failure, and short life could be a calamity. But if we look upon life as an eternal thing stretching far into pre-earth past and on into the eternal post-death future, then all happenings may be put into proper perspective.

Is there not wisdom in his giving us trials that we might rise above them, responsibilities that we might achieve, work to harden our muscles, sorrow to try our souls? Are we not permitted temptations to test our strength, sickness that we might learn patience, death that we might be immortalized and glorified?

. . . If mortality be the perfect state, then death would be a frustration, but the gospel teaches us there is no tragedy in death, but only in sin.

We know so little. Our judgement is so limited. We judge the Lord often with less wisdom than does our youngest child weigh our decisions. (Emphasis added.)

Oscar Wilde once wrote, "If God really wanted to punish us, he'd answer all our prayers." Imagine if there were no death, no sickness, no pain, no old age, no hard times, no trials of our faith, no misunderstandings, no errors, no mistakes. What kind of a life would it be? What would be the purpose of this earth life?

Think of the things people might pray for, and see if a culmination of all those desires granted upon the human race as a whole would not be misery itself. If there were no misery, could there be true joy? If there were no pain, could there be real gratitude for comfort? If there were no death, would we ever be raised in glorious resurrection with our Savior? If there were no struggle, would we ever grow? If we did not grow, would we ever reach the potential of becoming like him which once caused us to "shout for joy"?

As I am expressing feelings that seem in complete contradiction to one another—hurt and joy, pain and peace—throughout the experience of the accident, one might ask, "How can someone feel so much pain, and yet experience so much joy, peace, and happiness?" I'm not insinuating that the experience was easy after that, nor that it is easy today. I can imagine very few things that would be more difficult for me. I am merely trying to relate the significant contrasts—the joy, miracles, and light that were part of the experience during the darkest hours of my life.

When our hearts, minds, and bodies ache for understanding, the Lord stands ready to reveal his mighty arm in simple and majestic ways and our struggles bear uncommonly sweet fruit which can be produced in no other way

In reality, the Lord is building us. Carefully, meticulously, he goes over every aspect of our lives. He stretches us, molds us, and lifts us in ways only an all-knowing and loving God could. However, this process of growth is seldom painless, as C.S. Lewis noted:

> Imagine yourself living in a house. God comes to rebuild that house. At first, perhaps, you can understand what He is doing. He is getting the drains right and stopping the leaks in the roof and so on. You knew that those jobs needed doing and so you were not surprised. But presently he starts knocking the house about in a way that hurts and does not seem to make sense. What on earth is he up to? The explanation is that he is building quite a different house from the one you thought of—throwing out a new wing here, putting on an extra floor there, running up the towers, making courtyards. You thought you were going to be made into a decent little cottage; but he is building a palace.

Adversity is a common law of life. A law that we not only accepted before coming to this earth, but rejoiced over. Surely, under the divine tutelage of the Master, our substance will be slowly refined, strengthened, and tested, until our metal is declared "good."

The blacksmith pulls the metal from the burning red embers of the fire. The metal glows with heat as the hammer of the blacksmith comes down again and again with great force on the yielding form. Again, he places the metal into the flames and pounds his strength into the mass. The metal is beginning to show its shape. Slowly, the blacksmith works on the unrecognizable form, shaping it, molding it, changing it. Is it a plow, with which to turn the soil to feed the hungry? Is it a hinge, to swing the doors of opportunity back and forth? Is it a sword, to defend our liberty and freedom? In time the form begins to become distinguishable. Now comes the real test of the metal. Carrying the glowing form from the fire, the metal is doused into a cold bucket of water. Steam rises quickly from the cooling metal. The Master Craftsman pulls the form from the water and slowly studies it. Taking his hammer, he skillfully strikes the metal again. If the metal is good, it fills it purpose. If it is not, it breaks and is thrown into a growing heap of scrap metal, to await another day of trial.

We all feel the heat of adversity, cringe in pain at the banging of the hammer, and feel a change taking place inside our hearts and minds. Through this process I have felt the purpose of my existence, and can see a new form taking shape within me—a form which is imperative to the ultimate achievement of my dreams and desires. I only wait now to be dipped into the bucket of cold water, to have my steaming form lifted, examined, and judged. When that duty has been accomplished, I only pray that my metal is good enough to serve my Master. So long as I feel the heat of the fire and the pain of the hammer from time to time, and the flames again and again, I know that at least I have not been thrown into the scrap heap.

Still, the most powerful truth for me echoes in my heart and mind from that experience in the hospital: "Remember, Art, I told you I would never leave you to suffer alone. Art, when you suffer, I suffer. When you hurt, I hurt. And, when you cry, I cry. I promised, and I will not leave you now."

The Savior of us all walks this path of hurt, pain, and discouragement with us. He has suffered the stinging lash of the whip of my own adversity upon his back. One of the multitude of miracles revealed in my life came through the understanding of the promise he made to me that pain-filled day. It is as real for you as it is for me. That promise is eternal. It is for each of us. As Elisha of old, we never walk alone.

The prophet Elisha lived many, many years ago. It seemed as though Elisha had made a bitter enemy. You see, a few days earlier he had made the king of Syria very angry. He had told the king that if he did not repent the Lord would destroy him. The king vowed he would destroy Elisha for uttering those prophetic words of truth. Somehow, he believed that if he could destroy the messenger, he could eliminate the message, a lie taught only by the voice of Satan, himself.

On the morning that Elisha was to be murdered, the prophet was on a high mountain with a young man who was his servant. As a multitude of the king's men raced across the valley floor in chariots of war, the youth and Elisha silently watched the growing clouds of dust. The young man, fearful of the future, but with faith in his friend and companion, asked Elisha, "Master, how shall we do?"

In comforting assurance, Elisha gently answered, "Be not afraid, they that be with us are more than that be with them." The servant looked around bewildered for a moment. What did the prophet mean, "They that be with us are more than that be with them?" The young man could count—there were hundreds of soldiers of war, and only two of them.

Elisha, aware of the question in the servant's mind, turned his eyes heavenward and prayed aloud, "Lord, I pray thee, open his eyes that he may see." (2 Kings 6:17.) And then the young man's eyes were opened. The windows of heaven parted, and now, together, they watched concourses of angels racing forward on chariots of fire, all to aid a young man and an old prophet.

If the veil could be pushed back, if the windows of heaven

could be opened to our view, we, too, would see concourses of angels, friends, and family all rushing forward to lend us aid in our times of most desperate need. In the midst of them all stands a kind, wise loving Father and a merciful and compassionate Savior, who struggle and weep with us. As we understand this, we, too, in our hour of affliction can with confidence say, "Let this cup pass from me, but not my will, but thine be done." And then the learning begins.

I don't have all of the answers to the questions regarding "Why?" However, my mind and heart have been blessed with a sense of peace and comfort and I have come to realize that somewhere there are more good answers than there are questions. An endless array of books could not fully do those answers justice. In the quiet end to our own inquiries, we all must finally recognize that beyond our personal understanding there is still darkness and unanswered questions. Until the day when we all sit again at the feet of our Savior, we must tuck those questions away on a small shelf somewhere, satisfied with the knowledge of what we know and feel today. Someday, we'll know more.

> Not 'til the loom is silent
> And the shuttles cease to fly
> Will God unfold the pattern,
> And explain the reason why.
> The dark threads were as needful
> In the skillful weaver's hand,
> As the threads of Gold and Silver
> In the pattern that He planned.
>
> *(Author Unknown)*

After ten days in Las Vegas, four of which were spent in intensive care, I was taken by ambulance to a local airport. Gingerly they loaded my stretcher into a small single engine plane. They had done all they could for me in Las Vegas. My hope for recovery and rehabilitation now rested in San Jose, California, at the Santa Clara Valley Medical Center.

The small plane taxied the runway and we lifted off. The pilot banked the plane gently to the right to give me my last look at Las Vegas, the place of my "new birth," and then we headed west toward new horizons.

You can carry a pack
If it's strapped to your back;
You can carry a weight in your hands.
You can carry a bundle
On top of your head,
As they do in other lands.
A load is light
If you carry it right.
Though it weighs as much as a boulder;
But a tiny chip
Is too heavy to bear
If you carry it on your shoulders.

(Author Unknown)

Chapter Four
A Burden Too Heavy

Valley Medical Center was a county-run facility. It wasn't the nicest, and wouldn't win any awards for the way it smelled, but it was among the best when it came to spinal cord injuries. That was their specialty.

The floors were yellowing linoleum leading to walls painted an awful mint green color. My whole room hummed as doctors, nurses, and attendants busily made their way in and out of the room seeing to their responsibilities. As doctors came to my bed, they would look here, poke there, ask me if I could feel this or that, and then hurry out again. I soon learned that the constant flow of activity in the new hospital was the norm, day and night. At least every two hours around the clock for the next three and a half months, somebody would wake me to take my blood pressure, temperature, and vital signs. If sleep and good rest were what I needed, I had come to the wrong place.

However, in terms of people knowing what to do and how to do it, there seemed to be a world of difference between them and the hospital staff in Las Vegas. I felt more comfortable in this new setting, but I still felt fear and anxiety. What would be expected of me? What if I didn't get any better or stronger? What would my future hold?

Dallas had flown to Utah for a few days to pack and return permanently to San Jose, and so I was without my sweetheart for the first time since the accident, and I felt a part of me was missing. But I was back in my hometown, among friends again. Regardless of the anxiety of an uncertain future, being in my hometown brought a lot of comfort.

Soon they had me settled into a new intensive care room along with three other patients whom I rarely saw because they usually kept the curtains drawn around my bed. However, I could often hear and sense them. On occasion, I could hear a patient talking bitterly to family, friends, and nurses— sometimes striking out with harsh words at those who were trying to care for their needs. Others were more gracious, but said little or nothing to anyone. Late at night it was not uncommon to hear one of them crying himself to sleep. The nights were lonely. Even with the constant flow of activity all around, one felt very much alone.

My new doctor came in and introduced himself as Dr. Kelly. He had a strong Irish accent and was difficult to understand. I could tell he was a leader among the other doctors and his presence commanded respect. He was a man well-acquainted with the pain and suffering of others. He had assisted thousands of unfortunate people suffering from spinal cord injuries. He had many notable and good qualities as a doctor. However, I would soon learn that tact and sensitivity were not among them. To express it mildly, his bedside manner was awful. I soon discovered how easy it was to harbor feelings of resentment and anger for the emotional and physical pain this doctor brought to me and to my family.

Within the first couple of days during my stay at Valley Medical Hospital, Doctor Kelly called a special family conference. He outlined some of the new policies at the hospital and related how he saw the future for all of us. He also announced his personal plan of action for me. None of his words left a whole lot of hope or good feelings. To begin with, visiting hours were strictly limited and were to be adhered to, regardless of any special needs. Next, it was to be understood that I would never walk again—period! I would be required to have constant help for the rest of my life. I would always be in a wheelchair so we might as well get used to that fact. There was to be no more discussion of walking. Finally, I would begin therapy as soon as I could get up from my bed, which would require him to install a halo brace on me within the next couple of days. Our hearts became heavy, and his words created feelings of discouragement and frustration. I understood and respected his honesty. However, it was hard to forgive his insensitivity to our feelings, and the lack of attention he paid to the questions, ideas, and suggestions of those who wanted to help and who needed to understand.

My mother seemed to be the most adversely affected by the conference, and suddenly I was glad that Dallas was far away. Here are some of my mother's words as she recorded them in her journal:

> Dr. Kelly called six of us, including Art, into a very small room, for consultation. He explained Art's condition. We asked questions. He said Art's injury was "complete." He said Art would never walk again; that he would be a quadriplegic for the rest of his life.
>
> My emotions raged within me. Brother Carter (our home teacher) comforted me with a hand on my shoulder, but he soon had to leave the room to prevent himself from passing out. The experience was too traumatic and the news devastating. I could hardly wait to get out of that room! I felt

absolutely no respect for Dr. Kelly and I hated that place! My dear friend, Anne Day, comforted me in the open hallway as I cried on her shoulder for a long time. It was as though my whole world had been shattered.

For ten days I had prayed and fasted for faith and strength, and my prayers had been answered. Everything about the flight to San Jose had made it an exciting day. We all felt good about everything; our faith was high. But, suddenly my faith felt shattered like a broken light bulb. I cried for hours. I couldn't even go back into the ICU room to see Art. I didn't want him to know I was angry and crying. I felt so empty—yet full of rage, hurt, and fear. I had stayed with Art twenty-four hours a day for ten days. Now I couldn't even tell him goodnight. Anne, a registered nurse and a friend of the family since Art's birth, assured me she would stay with him as long as he needed her—all night, if necessary. Everyone insisted I get out of there. I couldn't stop crying!

Dad took me to dinner. I wasn't hungry, but I needed food as I hadn't eaten for twelve hours. I was still crying. The next morning I cooked breakfast for Dad and saw him off to work. We prayed together before he left. My visiting teacher and friends called to arrange dinners to be brought in for the family, and to see if I needed help with anything. I was still crying. In the early afternoon, I went to bed. I couldn't even talk to anyone without crying; I fell apart every time I tried to say anything to anyone. My faith had been shattered and I felt great fear and uncertainty. By 4 o'clock, I was ready to drive to San Jose. I was exhausted and miserably sleepy, but I had to go. I couldn't bear *not* to be at the hospital.

After a visit with Art, I felt much better. He was in good spirits. He felt good about his first 24 hours of care at Valley Medical. It was certainly far different than the hospital in Las

Vegas where they had a shortage of experienced nurses. Art's faith had *not* been shattered. His faith and ever-bright spirit strengthened me and those who were with him.

Have you ever seen a halo? Well, the halo I am referring to is not the kind we typically think of encircling the heads of saints and angels. I am speaking of a halo brace used in hospitals. Believe me, there is absolutely nothing angelic about a halo brace.

At first, when I heard Dr. Kelly wanted me to wear a halo brace, I objected. I saw little need to wear one of those hideous things. However, he insisted it was in my best interest to have one put on. I was told that with the halo brace I'd be able to get up into a wheelchair and begin therapy and rehabilitation immediately. I still hesitated. Unless you've seen a halo brace, you may have a hard time understanding why I would be so reluctant.

The halo brace starts with a large breast plate made of plastic and lined with sheepskin to keep the plastic from irritating the skin. Steel bars are attached to the chest plate and extend up and over the shoulders and then down the back. From the bars over the shoulders, another steel bar goes up along each side of the head. This bar is connected to the infamous halo. The halo is a flat metal bar about one-inch wide, that completely encircles the head from front to back. If you've got that pictured, then imagine four three-inch bolts, pointed sharply at the end, screwed into the patient's head, two in the front and two in the back, to hold the halo in place. Gruesome, isn't it?

It almost sounds medieval. The very thought of it is still frightening to me. Even today I get cold chills and feel weak when I see one. The halo brace is offensive to look at, to say the least, and I often wondered how so many friends and family could still come visit with me when I was wearing this hideous "cage."

You bet I hesitated having it put on! In retrospect, if I had the decision to make again, taking into account the excruciating pain, discomfort, inability to rest, and the awful look of the whole thing, I would have definitely said no. Although the brace is essential in some cases, as it turned out, the halo brace would not have been a necessity for me after all.

When the doctor's assistant carried the halo brace into the room, my heart jumped. Silently, I prayed for the strength it would take to endure the installation process. I knew those three-inch bolts would have to be manually screwed into my skull through my forehead and just behind my ears. What I didn't know was that it would be done with no anesthesia—no pain killer that was the least bit effective.

The doctor did inject medication in each of the four areas the bolts were to enter, but whatever it was supposed to do, it didn't. As they strapped the breastplate into place and adjusted the hardware, one of the bolts scraped across an area of the forehead where they were to be inserted. I could feel it! I thought that area was was supposed to be numb from the "pain killer," but it wasn't. I told Dr. Kelly I could still feel it as though no anesthesia had been given. He continued adjusting the chest plate and hardware. I told him again, this time with panic in my voice. "Please," I begged him, "wait until the anesthesia has taken effect." Ignoring my pleas, he had somebody hold my arms down, and picked up the instrument to be used for screwing in the bolts.

Before beginning the arduously slow process of inserting them into my skull, he commented coldly, "It's supposed to hurt. It'll go away." The process began.

Never have I felt anything so painful in all my life. I personally cannot conceive of anything more excruciating. I felt as though an explosion was going off inside my body. I felt I could not contain the pain. I wanted to die. I wanted life to stop right where I lay. Surely, I could not suffer this intensely and survive. Tears were forced from the corners of my eyes. As my face became contorted and wreathed in pain, I saw a vision I have never forgotten. I saw a man already weak from a terrible beating being laid on a cross with his arms and legs outstretched. The rough surface of the wooden crucifix cut into his already beaten and bloodied back. With vivid and intense detail, I saw men drive nails into the quivering and innocent flesh of his hands and feet, and a God suffered and eventually died. In the middle of all my pain, the bright lights, and the voices, I heard a soft voice within me echo, "Art, you're not alone. I know this is hard. Please, hold on. I am here." Tears rolled down my face. Eternity surely could not have seemed longer. I felt the horror would never end.

"Go ahead, scream if you need to," Dr. Kelly commented, as he continued. I would have, but I couldn't. I opened my mouth and nothing would come out. My vision began to go black. I knew my body was beginning to go into shock; I had been there before. Then it was over. The doctors backed away from me to observe the situation. I heard Dr. Kelly's voice say casually, "He's in some pain. I think we need to give him something for it." My world was spinning and I lost all recognition of what was going on around me. Everything went dark.

I wore that halo brace for the next ten weeks and I looked hideous. Despite the "new look," I was able to begin my rehabilitation program, although the size and weight of the brace made exercise difficult and cumbersome. Sleeping at night was strained at best. It felt as though I were sleeping on pencils. Headaches became a daily event. My head felt like a bruised melon in a closed vise.

Three times each day my thong sights had to be sterilized in order to avoid infection where the bolts entered my forehead. It was never a comfortable procedure, and usually I just gritted my teeth and endured. Many of the nurses and attendants were sensitive to my discomfort and did everything they could to make the experience less painful for me. These were special people who, even though they lived amongst pain every day, had managed to stay sensitive to their patients and had learned to persistently exercise compassion.

Then there was one male nurse who was different than the rest. His eyes were dark and deep set. He always reeked of cigarette smoke and sometimes alcohol. He was generally an unclean person with mind and language to match. His life seemed entirely void of anything called compassion.

To the contrary, he seemed to enjoy seeing others in pain. For some sadistic reason, he would think it was funny if I jerked back in pain when he hit a sensitive spot or if he scrubbed too hard. As the weeks went on, his cleaning of my wounds became more and more rough, which increased the pain of the experience a great deal.

Finally one day, when I felt I had taken as much as I could, I asked him to let me have someone else clean my thong sites. He refused, calling me names which were both cruel and inappropriate. When I told him I would not allow him to scrub me again without seeing my doctor, he laughed, held my weak arms to the bed, and scrubbed mercilessly.

It is hard to imagine that kind of cruelty. I find it difficult to believe it ever happened. I saw the cold and dark nature of a "natural man," and shuddered. How does one forgive such things? How was I to resolve these feelings of hurt and anger?

The words of my mission president softly repeated themselves in my mind many times, "Those who cannot forgive another burn the very bridges over which they themselves must someday cross."

To hate would be so easy. But when the poison of anger and spite begin to course through my veins for a doctor, a male nurse, or others who inflicted unnecessary pain and agony, my heart cries against it. While at the mercy of other's actions, I experienced a sublime and intimate encounter with my Savior. His perfect love and compassion flowed over my mind and heart in such a unique and powerful way as to permanently imbue its influence upon my life. To hate a doctor or spite a member of his staff would negate and mock the effects and wonder of that miracle which the Lord himself bestowed.

Elder Thomas S. Monson, recently declared of Christ, "He commands, and to those who obey him, whether they be wise or simple, he will *reveal himself in the toils, the conflicts, and the sufferings which they shall pass through in his fellowship; and they shall learn in their own experience who he is.*" (emphasis added.) Despite the difficulty of the requirement, he has commanded us, "Love your enemies, bless them that curse you, do good to them that hate you, and pray for them which despitefully use you, and persecute you." (Matt. 5:44.) While reflecting on the intimate experiences of coming to know, in a powerful way, who my Savior is, I learned to quietly pray, "God, bless Dr. Kelly." And the venom of hate was gone. It is a venom, because those who are poisoned by it find the road to their own happiness and peace eroded and washed away. While those who learn to love and pray, rather than hate and spite, will find the Savior and "learn in their own experience who he is." Let me share with you a parable I wrote about this.

A man walked along a dusty highway. In a short while he came upon a small community. He was hot, tired, and thirsty, and began to search for an appropriate resting place.

In his search, he found a group of people who were unwilling to help him, intolerant, and selfish. Rather than assist in tending to his needs, they sent him on his way unsatisfied. The man stood at the far edge of town. Looking back, he gently picked up a rough stone from the highway, placed it in his bag, and said to himself, "I'll remember this."

As he traveled farther, he came upon a gathering of people beside the highway. They all wore the finest clothing and jewelry that one could possibly desire. The man had traveled long without companionship and was hungry for human conversation. He would rest here a while, acquaint himself with these good people, and then be on his way again.

As he approached, someone from the group caught a glimpse of him and began to laugh and point. The others looked, and they too laughed at the man whose clothes were torn, dirty, and old. The man hung his head and traveled on. A short distance later, he reached down and picked up another stone, this one larger than the first, and placed it in his bag, saying, "I'll remember this."

Finally, unable to go any farther without rest, he sat beneath the shade of a big tree and slept. Upon awakening, he found that someone had stolen all his possessions except the bag with the stones. Quickly, he found another large stone and placed it in his bag and moved on, repeating, "I'll remember this." These stones became the only thing that this man carried. Each day, he took his stones from the bag to count and clean them. Each day, as he suffered more and more injustices, cruelties, and unfairness, he gathered more stones to add to his growing collection.

At last, one day, he found he could go no farther. His bag was full and heavy and difficult to bear. However, his stones had become too important for him now to leave them. They had become the center of his life. He cared for these stones, talked of them in his conversations with others, and used them to justify his own acts of misbehavior. What would he do without them?

So he continued to carry them. His back became bent with the weight as he strained through life collecting these stones. His eyes became cynical, and his body showed signs of early aging. But he could not give up his stones. Finally, in frustration he died.

How different would his life have been without those stones? How much easier would his way have been and how much lighter his load to bear?

We all carry a burden in this life. Life is hard for each of us. However, those who collect stones of injustice, insensitivity and wrongdoing, saying, "I'll remember this," end up carrying far greater weights than the people who have done them wrong.

This was an additional weight I could not afford to bear. The Savior said, "Come unto me, all ye that labour and are heavy laden, and I will give you rest . . . . For my yoke is easy, and my burden is light." (Matthew 11:28, 30.)

The weight of my adversities was already heavy enough. I could not consider the thought of adding more by carrying the burden of other's unkindness or injustice as well. In my heart I prayed that God Almighty would help me forgive these people I felt had done me wrong. I prayed that the weight of their sins, of their lack of compassion, would be removed from me. I desired to leave their stones along the highway where I had found them.

I do not mean to imply that this was easy—to the contrary. I found it necessary to continually persist in these pleadings with the Lord, expressing and further developing my desire to eventually be free from hate and anger. Then one day, as I evaluated the things I was carrying in my bag of life, I discovered that the stones of resentment, anger, and spite were gone. I smiled, and thanked God who promised me "rest unto [my] soul" if I would follow him.

As I explain the cause of my accident, people will often ask, "What happened to, John, the driver?" To some it would seem fair and just if he had sustained greater injuries than I did. Physically, John was not badly hurt. He received only minor cuts, abrasions, and a puncture wound in his bicep. The next question some ask is, "How do you feel about John—the guy who did this to you?" That is an awkward question, because John never *did* anything to *me*. It was an accident—not negligence or disregard or insensitivity; just an accident. The "tragedy" the accident created in my life is no more distressing and painful than the nightmare John still lives with today.

Shortly after I was released from the hospital in April, Dallas and I went to the Salt Lake Temple to witness the marriage of Dallas's brother, Scott. Scott and I had become good friends over the years, and it was a special time for all of us. John was also there. John and Scott were new friends and he desired to share in the special event.

The ceremony was beautiful and touching. Dallas and I looked across at each other with tear-filled eyes as the ceremony began. We were both reminded of our own interrupted marriage plans. A long and flowing white dress still hung, unused and covered with plastic, in Dallas's closet back home. More than anything right now, we wanted to be sealed together forever through sacred marriage covenants. However, we knew we'd have to wait. Waiting had become more and more familiar to us.

I am not sure if John saw our eyes and interpreted the hurt and emotional pain of the moment, or whether he had just been touched by the whole experience himself, but, silently, he began to cry. He continued to cry to himself in the corner of the sealing room for the rest of the ceremony. When it was over, he excused himself to another room of the temple. We followed, hoping to give him comfort.

There, in the quiet solitude and confines of the Lord's House, he wept uncontrollably. His whole body jerked as he gasped for air, and then cried some more. I have never seen anyone weep with such intensity and pain. He seemed completely overwhelmed. We tried to help restore him, to assure and comfort him. We could not. His heart was breaking—a heart he thought had been healed months ago. John and I learned then that it would be difficult for his broken heart to ever really mend, except through the power and influence of the Savior's love. You see, it should have been *my* wedding he was attending. It should have been the day Dallas and I longed for. We should have been kneeling across that altar, only now I couldn't even kneel.

As many times as I tell him that the accident was not his fault, that he in no way intended to harm me and therefore is not to be blamed or held responsible, the nightmare of what happened continues to haunt him. To think you have brought this kind of pain, trauma, and adversity into someone's life, even though you would never choose to do so, is extremely difficult to live with.

Maybe it is appropriate that people continue to ask me how I feel about John. I will continue to respond, "I love him. He's my friend." Some have asked how long it took for me to forgive him. My answer is, "I never felt I had anything to forgive him for in the first place." I can tell you one thing for sure: I thank God I am in my shoes today, and not his. I don't know if I could have faced so bravely the nightmare he has had to endure. His burden, too, has been heavy.

As many friends heard of my accident and rushed to my side, all too often John's pain went unnoticed. However, John did not spend his time feeling sorry for himself. Day and night he stayed by my bedside. He helped me, he read to me, he brought me comfort. During those first ten days, I saw into John's big heart. If you could have given him the chance, he surely would have traded places with me. Does a man with a heart like that need forgiveness from me? I don't think so. There is nothing to forgive.

Isn't it strange, that princes and kings
And clowns that caper in sawdust rings,
And common people like you and me
Are builders for eternity?
And each is given a bag of tools,
A shapeless mass, and a book of rules;
And each must make 'ere life is flown
A stumbling block, or a stepping stone.

(Author Unknown)

Chapter Five
My Bag of Tools

I sat in front of my breakfast and looked at my new challenge. As a quadriplegic, I had to re-learn many things in my life, and eating breakfast was one of them. I know eating breakfast doesn't sound like that hard of a task. Well, the food wasn't my problem; it was getting the food to my mouth successfully that was the challenge. My hands were paralyzed, so I had to use a special instrument to help me pick up my fork and raise it to my mouth. To complicate matters, I was required to wear a chest strap to keep me from falling out of my chair. Wearing my steel halo brace caused me to be extremely top heavy. Without the use of my stomach muscles to help keep me upright and with no use of my neck and head to assist in balancing me, I was strapped into my chair for my own safety.

I had two requests of my therapist that morning. The first was that I wanted to eat breakfast by myself. She agreed to give me thirty minutes. My second request took her even more by surprise. Tired of wearing a restraining belt around my chest wherever I went, I was anxious to try life without it. The therapist responded, "Are you absolutely sure?" Smiling, I calmly assured her of my desire. Hesitantly, she unfastened the strap and left.

I vividly remember what I was going to eat that morning. It was scrambled eggs with a hot biscuit. Reaching for the fork, I maneuvered it between my fingers to try and get some kind of a hold on it. Once it felt reasonably secure, I lifted it toward the plate. With my arm extended directly in front of me I was presented with a balance problem I had not anticipated. Even though my sense of equilibrium was not completely accurate, I recognized from the sight of the fast approaching plate of food that I was falling forward. Having little use of my weak arms, any attempt to stop myself was futile. With the weight of the halo brace pushing me forward, my face landed squarely in my plate of food.

I listened for a moment to see if I could hear anyone. Then, using my weakened arms, I tried to sit myself up again. That option was out. I was stuck right there, face down in my scrambled eggs. Now, with a whole new perspective on the four basic food groups, two thoughts crossed my mind. The first was that this was probably going to be one of the longest twenty-eight minutes of my life. The second thought was that I probably wouldn't get into a more advantageous position for eating for a long time . . . so I ate my breakfast. I've never had the same appreciation for scrambled eggs and biscuits since!

At the time we had agreed upon, the therapist walked back into the room, and seeing my situation, quickly rushed to my side and pulled me out of my plate. I showed obvious relief to have my vision of the room restored. The therapist, noticing that the plate was shiny and clean, excitedly asked me, "Well, how did you do?"

"All right," I responded, "It was a little tough getting the butter on the biscuit, but I did okay!"

As my new life began, my days and hours became filled with re-learning the essentials of life. It was like being a child again who first learns to pick things up, then manipulate them, then to crawl, walk, and run. I was a child starting all over again.

More than two thousand years ago, Aristotle wrote,

"Learning is not child's play; we cannot learn without pain." Learning is one of the primary reasons you and I are here. Growing beyond our childhood years, we sometimes begin to avoid the learning process, comfortable with the skills and knowledge we have already acquired. There is great danger in that. To learn is to grow; to grow is to change; and to change is the greatest miracle ever endowed on the human race. To avoid pain is to resist the learning processes and frustrate our own miracle. While for many the miracle which happens in a moment is appropriate, many more are blessed through the miracle of time and struggle to enhance and facilitate the learning, becoming process.

In working through and struggling in our own unique sceneario of adversity, we are each given a "custom-designed bag of tools." These tools are ours to use in the process of cultivating and harvesting the fruits of our pain. Some of these tools are: talents, faith, optimism, patience, virtue, knowledge, love, gifts of the Spirit, family, prayer, and service. All of them can be used to create the "good" which comes from all things to those who "love God." (Romans 8:28.)

New tools are acquired and old tools are enhanced as we use them during our most difficult hours. Without the weight and burden of trials, valuable tools necessary to produce real happiness and enrich our life's experience go unused, get tarnished, and eventually are lost. When we take what tools we have and dig them deep into the rich soil of our own struggles, the learning process starts and we begin to grow. Looking carefully through my own unique bag of tools, I was ready to learn.

Being paralyzed, I had lost all muscle function from the chest down, including my stomach and leg muscles. I also lost the use of my hands and much of the use of my arms—the muscles in the shoulders and arms were weak and I had no use of the right tricep. During those first days and weeks, my body became weak and thin. Before the accident, I had weighed as much as 168 pounds, standing six feet tall. Within a very short period of time, I lost forty-eight pounds. With those pounds, I also lost much of my physical strength—even in the few muscles that continued to work.

Each morning a therapist would come to my bedside and stretch my legs, arms, and hands to keep them as limber as possible. Beginning after breakfast, I would work with different therapists. Sometimes it was frustrating and discouraging. I felt foolish and angry for not being able to do even the simplest things. At one time they had me practicing for an hour each day stacking children's building blocks. You know the ones—they have the alphabet on the sides with pictures of ducks and lambs. The exercise was to improve my hand dexterity and to teach me to pick up small objects again. Hour after hour I struggled to make my hands and arms useful and productive again. At times I sat and stared at the hands that once did so much, so easily. Now they labored over the weight and challenge of picking up a tiny building block from a table.

Later, I learned to shakingly hold a felt-tip pen between my stiff fingers and make marks on a piece of paper. After hours and days of effort, I began to form those marks into letters and words and then sentences. Each day, for an hour, I would struggle to write thank you notes and brief letters. Each letter was barely legible. Before my accident, I had beautiful, flowing handwriting. Now, I had the handwriting of a hundred year-old man. Each letter of the alphabet took effort and concentration. A short note took as long as an hour or two, even though it consisted of only four or five sentences.

Later, finger splints were made for me so I could learn to

type again. Before the accident, I had been able to type sixty words-per-minute. Now, I had to slowly peck out each letter with exacting effort and deliberation. I persisted in practicing, though. Even after leaving the hospital, I continued to type as often as I could, sometimes for hours at a time. If you were to watch me today, you would see me typing at speeds of forty words per minute and better, using only two fingers.

During other parts of the day, I spent time lying on large mats that were raised about eighteen inches off the floor. Under the direction of a therapist, I was being taught how to roll over again. I know that sounds kind of silly, but these are just examples of the things that I re-learned through hours of work and practice. They also taught me to get up on my elbows and drag my body from one end of the mat to the other. At first, I could barely even move my body at all. Eventually, I progressed to moving much farther.

Sometimes, it was difficult to see any long-term advantage that could come from my struggles. I questioned the therapist, asking why I needed to learn to drag myself around a mat. She thought for a moment, then with a smile on her face that showed a sense of pride in her well-thought-out answer, she said, "In case there is a fire at night, you can roll out of bed onto the floor and drag yourself to safety."

Sounded good, but I had one more question, "How do I get the door open once I drag myself all the way across the room?" That ended that therapy class for the day.

Let me describe my least favorite part of therapy. Suddenly my breathing would become labored and heavy. Each breath came with work and effort. I focused as much as I could on objects across the room. Before I knew it the objects were becoming fuzzy and unclear. Black spots began to appear and my head started to throb. I tried to breathe again but I felt I was drifting away. The edges of my vision became dark. It seemed the room was filled with thick, black smoke. Then everything went black.

I had no sensation of where I was, where I had been, or how long I had been gone. At first I could hear voices, then light began to fill my vision again, and I could see. My normal breathing returned, and even though my head was splitting wide with a headache, I could see the lights of the ceiling clearly.

I was on the infamous tilt table—a padded table with straps at the head and foot. In efforts to keep my blood pressure and circulation functioning properly, I used the tilt table daily.

Lying on my back, they would strap my knees and chest down. Then, with a therapist at the controls, they would hydraulically lift the table at the head until it was slightly inclined. I would fight my need for oxygen, breathing heavily, and eventually I would lose all oxygen-carrying blood to the brain, causing me to pass out. Then I'd be lowered, brought back to reality, and then raised again. This was done every day for weeks, tilting the table farther and farther, as they tried to build my endurance to a point where I could maintain a standing position. That feeling of passing out was something I never quite got used to, although I certainly became familiar with the aspirin bottle.

Later, after I had been in the hospital for a while, I was challenged with even more creative means of adapting to life's new circumstances. Believe it or not, they brought me to the kitchen. This is what they called occupational therapy, although, I had a difficult time imagining anyone hiring me as a cook. That could be dangerous! However, I thought I would humor them nonetheless.

They began by having me create a simple peanut butter sandwich. I say "create," because that's the best word to describe what it looked like after I was done trying to get the peanut butter off the knife and onto the bread. Scrambled sandwich would have been more appropriate. However, I swallowed my pride, along with the sandwich, to prove my self-reliance.

Then came the fun part. They actually wanted me to bake a cake. I said, "No problem." I began by tearing off the top of the cake mix box with my teeth. Luckily, I got at least half of the mix into the bowl. The therapist just watched and smiled. I was glad to see that at least she was enjoying this. Then came the tricky part. How does a guy with limited use of his hands and arms gently crack an egg into a bowl without getting bits of shell into the mix? I thought for a moment. A smile spread across my face. I gently cradled the egg in the palm of my hand, raised it above the bowl, and slammed it into the mix! It broke all right! Egg and mix went everywhere—all over me, the table and even the therapist. I think she lost all hope of me becoming a cook. By the way, the cake was delicious, as long as you watched out for those little white shells.

Hard work was the order of every day at the medical center. However, there were those times when I was able to escape it. After one particularly grueling morning of therapy, I decided to find a way to avoid the afternoon session. Immediately following my lunch, I headed slowly for the door which led to an outside patio area. I was confident I could find peace and seclusion there. Once on the patio, I felt I would be more difficult to find if I went around to the side of the building than if I just sat there outside the door.

The sidewalk was a little sloped and listed to the left, but confident from my hours of therapy, I began my descent. As I moved down the sidewalk, my speed began to increase measurably. My weak arms struggled to keep my chair under control. I was definitely going to crash! Having a desire to avoid as many injuries as possible, I steered my wheelchair in the direction of a large, soft-looking bush. Off the sidewalk I went, crashing face first into the large, green bush that was absolutely nothing close to soft. Although I remained in the chair, I was now entangled in the branches and leaves of my new foliage-friend, and getting back on the sidewalk by my own power would be impossible.

I was in that awkward position for at least ten minutes before I heard someone's footsteps approaching. They couldn't see me, but at least this would be my chance. I cried out, "Hey you!" The footsteps stopped. I could tell the person was looking around. The footsteps began again, this time headed away from where I was. I cried more desperately, "Hey! I need some help." The footsteps again stopped. Then I realized why the hesitation. The building next to me was big and white, with bars on the windows, and a sign which read, "Mental Institution." I laughed to myself; I would have hesitated, too. I had to be more convincing. "It's me. I'm in a wheelchair and I'm over here in a bush. I'm stuck. Can you help?" Now the stranger came willingly, and with a somewhat embarrassed look, helped me from my prison of foliage. I headed quickly back to therapy. At least there I was safe!

A week later, with the memory of my "bush experience" dimming, it was time to plan another escape. Waiting until after the dinner hour, Dallas, John, and I made our way to the already dark parking lot. We had made it appear as though they were simply taking me for a relaxing after-dinner stroll through the hospital; then we suddenly darted through a side door leading to freedom. If I had been wearing a black hat with a scarf drawn over my nose and mouth, I would have felt no more like Butch Cassidy or the Sundance Kid than I did then.

Loading me into a car was the biggest joke of all. I was still wearing that hideous-looking halo brace which kept me from bending my upper body, head, or neck. John's small Volkswagen presented quite a problem—little door, long person who doesn't bend. Using John's strength and Dallas's creativity, they pushed and pulled until I finally found myself in the front seat. It felt strange to be in a car again. It had been months since I had been away from hospitals. It was a cold evening, but I was dressed warmly.

John carefully and slowly drove the car down the street. Before long we pulled into the theatre's parking lot. We were going to the movies—John, Dallas, and Frankenstein. You have to understand how ridiculous I looked. Wearing the halo brace, I looked gruesome. We tried to cover up the metal with the hood of my sweatshirt. However, the bolts that came from the forehead area protruded out from the hood and the steel halo shone, even in the moonlight. Luckily, it was not a busy night, but the doorman had a hard time not revealing his thoughts as he stared at me. I looked like I was straight from some kind of torture chamber in a horror movie.

The movie was fun. We laughed together, and for a moment I forgot I had to go back. However, as we pulled into the hospital parking lot and I looked up at the dark building looming in the night, the reality of my days ahead became very clear again.

A lot of physical, mental, and spiritual progress was made in that hospital. When I arrived there from Las Vegas, I was capable of doing nothing. My body was weak and useless. The contents of my own personal bag of tools was limited. As I worked day after day I began to learn new things. New strength and endurance for pain and struggle were built to higher levels. Even with all of the physical progress, however, to the average observer I was still capable of doing nothing. But I had actually made giant steps forward. I was involved in the struggle of my life. Some people bet that I would lose, others cheered me on.

As for me, I knew I had to win no matter what the price or how long the road. And so each day, I grimaced at the pain of learning, smiled at Fate, and defeated her. Given the gift of time and struggle, while utilizing and discovering the tools within my reach, the Lord's mighty arm was being revealed and a miracle was happening!

By the time I left the hospital, I was far beyond what the doctors had anticipated or planned. Dr. Kelly, who arrogantly announced that he had never been wrong in over 3,000 cases, reluctantly agreed that my condition had changed dramatically. He used the word "dramatically." I would have said the change was miraculous.

Even today the miracle goes on. Only a couple of years ago I added another name to my growing list of doctors who had treated me. After a complete examination and a battery of tests, he looked over my previous medical records which revealed Dr. Kelly's original diagnosis. He broke into a smile and announced, "I am pleased to report, Art, that this first diagnosis is entirely wrong. It leaves no medical explanation for the outstanding progress you've made."

Where my arms before had been completely helpless, now I could use them to lift small objects and help me balance. Where my hands had been unproductive, now I employed them to get the little things I needed. Where before I didn't have the strength to push my wheelchair forward even an inch, now I could move slowly down a smooth hallway.

You might say I experienced optimum benefits from the quality program of therapy the hospital offered me, but I say God opened the windows of heaven and blessed me. He gave me strength to go on and the determination to fight and win. He endowed me with optimism and a sense of humor to lift my spirits even in that dark abyss. With every inch of progress I made, I thanked God who gave me hope, strength, and desire. There is purpose in waiting; there is power in time. And while he has blessed me with the miracle of time, I continue to learn, grow, and change. My dreams are being fulfilled, not in spite of my struggles, but because of them.

When good friends walk beside us
On the trails that we must keep,
Our burdens seem less heavy
And the hills are not so steep.
The weary miles pass swiftly
Taken in a joyous stride,
And all the world seems brighter
When friends walk by our side.

(Author Unknown)

Chapter Six
Friends By My Side

The walls were decorated with signs declaring, "Get Well, Art." Colorful cards and messages were taped everywhere. The shelves above my bed were sagging under the weight of dozens of inspiring and motivational books. A large mural-type picture of the Savior stretched above the bed. Flowers and green plants seemed to be growing from every corner. Balloons with streamers ascended from my headboard.

These were all signs of friends and family who came to visit, lift, and inspire me. At first we kept a daily log of every person who came. The list became unbelievably long. In the first few weeks as many as thirty to forty visited per day. It is difficult to imagine the outpouring of love, compassion and strength they brought with them. It was easy to feel loved.

Distance made little difference. Many friends made weekly, and even daily trips from as far away as Hollister, California. It was a distance of better than sixty miles. Many who came were young people, and even children. Each person brought with them gifts of the heart and spirit which could never be repaid. Many never realized the great impact their visits had on my progress, attitude, and determination. Yet, they came again and again.

Even before my accident, the Lord prepared the hearts and minds of those I loved. It is easy to see how, to the Lord, life is one eternal round. Everything is seen by his watchful eye, everything is known through his omniscience. In those early hours of our trip to Utah, as I was driving into the darkness, many miles away in the quiet of her home and the warmth of her bed, Dallas's mother, Rae, was kept awake by some foreboding and disturbing feelings. Somehow, she felt that I was in danger. Slipping from the warmth of the bed onto the cold floor, she softly prayed. A feeling of peace and calm assured her that even though danger might be imminent, God was with us. Resolving to begin a fast for our safety, she climbed back into bed, and fell back into the world of sleep.

Others were also given a glimpse into the future. On Christmas day, as relatives and friends visited Dallas's home, her Uncle Bill was there. While they visited by the fire, Dallas came bounding into the room with some friends. She lovingly greeted her Uncle and declared she was on her way to a friend's house for further Christmas festivities. A shadow suddenly loomed in Uncle Bill's mind and these words were etched: "I hope Dallas can withstand the pain that will shortly come into her life."

All things are known by an omniscient Lord. Because he knows all things, he can prepare the hearts and minds of others who will need to help, lift, inspire, and comfort those who are hurting. Often, the Lord's arm is revealed through the sacrifice, compassion and toil of others.

If the Lord healed all sickness, and prevented every tragedy, you and I would lose the great miracles which occur when we lose ourselves in the service of others. Certain miracles in our own lives and in the lives of others would be impossible without the involvement of friends and "comrades in arms." Some miracles take time, the power of the Lord, *and* people who are willing to care and serve.

Often the service we render can change the condition and lighten the burden of our neighbor, but even more frequently, it changes *our* hearts and lightens *our* burdens. From the scriptures, the Lord declared, "but whosoever will lose his life, for my sake the same shall save it." (Luke 9:24.) When we assume the responsibility and privilege included in the covenant of baptism, to "bear one another's burdens that they may be light," (Mosiah 18:8.) our own burdens become less noticeable and we become partners with the Lord in making the "works of God manifest" in the lives of others.

Sometimes there is little we can do or say except to be there. Norman Hill once wrote the story of a little boy who was sent on an errand by his mother and took longer than expected. When he returned, his mother questioned him about the delay.

The boy responded, "I met another boy whose tricycle was broken and who was crying because he couldn't fix it. So I helped him."

"But you don't know how to fix a tricycle," his mother said curiously.

"No, I don't," the young boy said, "so I sat down and cried with him." (*When The Road Gets Rough*, Norman C. Hill, Bookcraft, 1986, p. 3.)

When compassion, empathy, and love are shared through selfless acts of human kindness and service, the seeds of miracles are planted. As Jesus stood outside the tomb of the dead Lazarus, he took compassion on the mourning Martha and Mary. Even though he had a perfect knowledge of the powerful miracle about to take place, the scriptures record that, "Jesus wept." (John 11:35.) He could have counseled, rebuked, taught, or expounded. He chose to weep; and the shortest verse within recorded scripture speaks more of the nature of Christ than a thousand parables.

While the seeming tragedy of my experience brought old friends and new to my side, it drove others away. Dramatic changes can sometimes scare even the truest friends into hiding. Tragedy is a difficult thing to face. In a moment, lives that once sang harmoniously together, now have no apparent rhythm. Even very intimate friends drift away. However, many times the emptiness is filled as new friends come to offer support during moments of desperate need.

The constant flow of friends seemed only to compliment the consistent staying strength of my family who were by my side day after day after day. If my friends stayed hours, my family stayed hundreds of hours. If my friends drove hundreds of miles, my family drove tens of hundreds of miles. They never gave up on me.

You might in your mind say, "Well, of course they didn't. What friends or family would?" I think you would be shocked to see the number of patients who suffered as I did in that hospital whose families *never* came. No friends visited. No flowers decorated their bedside tables. No cards colored the walls. These fellow-sufferers had been dealt a tremendous blow in their lives, and no one cared enough to share that weight with them. I felt for them.

However, I also understood the great weight and burden my family carried by being there for me. If you questioned them about that today they would all probably reply, "Oh, it was no big thing. We simply did what we needed to do." But, I saw their pain every day. I saw the emotions held back as they sat with me. I saw their enthusiasm as I learned how to wiggle my little finger again. I felt their hearts break again and again and again. But the Lord mended them, and my family and friends are still there for me today. Tragedy and pain have a way of cementing the ties of family unity in a unique and powerful way. By grasping the opportunity to love and serve me, my family now enjoys the miracle that comes when we learn to "lose ourselves."

For years, a favorite film of mine has been, *It's A Wonderful Life,* that Christmastime special starring Jimmy Stewart. It's the story of a man who spends his life helping others, but suffers a devastating financial setback later in his years. At this point he contemplates that perhaps life would have been better for himself and others if he had never been born. In the end, his friends gather from everywhere to help him in his hour of need. The conclusion always makes my eyes fill with tears as a book is opened and on the front inside cover is written, "No man has failed who has friends."

I don't mean to imply that I had spent any measure of my life serving my friends. However, I did love them, and they loved me. They saw me suffering, and rushed to provide comfort and peace. These special friends, I am sure, would render this outpouring of love and concern to anyone among them suffering under similar circumstances. I know this, because I have witnessed them in action before and since. This is the kind of love the Savior taught. And now they taught it to me. The seeds of their actions nourished optimism, good attitude, and constant growth in my own struggling life. They became a part of the miracle.

No man is an island. Many lives can be eternally affected by the events of one accident. One man in particular I saw changed was an older man, small in stature, rough in manner. I wondered if he had a heart. I had been on many a job site with him and he showed no personal interest in me. Sometimes I winced at his language. Yet, when he heard of my accident he came to see me.

I had thought of him as a hard and calloused man beyond

feelings and human emotion. However, that was not true the day he visited me. He came in while I was finishing a therapy class. From the corner of the room, he watched me struggle to do things that were so simple and easy a short time before. He was overcome. He began to cry like a child. Those who were with him tried to comfort him. When he finally had his emotions under control, he whispered, "May God bless. I will pray for you." And he left the hospital. A new man was being born.

In future months, as I saw him working at job sites, I saw a different demeanor. He spoke in gentle, respectful language. His eyes showed a new light which seemed to affect his entire behavior. A simple accident brought new perspective and feelings to a coarse man.

As I received visitors, many told me of their children's unrelenting desire to pray for me. They said their children would pray for me at every meal, family prayer, and bedtime. Months after I left the hospital, friends still told me of their children's prayers as they continued to humbly petition the Lord for me on a daily basis. It is no wonder the Lord said, "Suffer the little children to come unto me." Their faith was so simple, their requests being merely a matter of fact. The Lord heard the prayers of his little ones, and answered them. It is no wonder we are directed to become as little children.

My brother, Paul, had left on his mission only weeks before my accident. He had been called to serve in Seoul, South Korea. We were all so excited for him, but for me, personally, it was hard to see him leave. All our lives we had been such close friends. We did everything together. Even though I had many friends who were not a part of my family, my brother had always been my best friend. Now, he was leaving for two years.

Paul was in a language class when a message was delivered to his room. The message was, "You are to call your parents at once. There has been an emergency." What was it? What could it be? All of life's ugliest scenes passed before him as he made his way down the empty hallway of the MTC. Could it be Mom or Dad? Maybe Roger is hurt . . . again? He reached the phone. "Hello, Mom . . . this is Paul." Silence. "Mom?"

"Paul, it's your brother Art. He's been involved in a serious automobile accident. He's critically injured. His neck is broken and he may never walk again."

Paul relates that suddenly the receiver felt like a hundred pound barbell. He thought, "Art? That's impossible! After all we've been through? After the dozens of trips we made together across that desert? It can't be!"

But, it was. Paul cried that day as he, too, experienced a broken heart. Quickly, however, with his emotions barely under control, he rallied other missionaries, told the story of his brother, and invoked their faith and prayers. Humbly, earnestly, and with real Christlike love, missionaries knelt and prayed together for me. Even as I lay suffering some nine hours away, the Lord heard those prayers and answered them.

After I had been in the hospital for about five weeks, a silent wish came true for me. Paul would be leaving from the MTC for South Korea soon, and I was wishing I could see him before he left. Through the voice of a concerned and caring bishop, the MTC mission president heard of our family's struggle. He arranged for Paul to catch a flight from Salt Lake City, Utah, to the hospital in San Jose, California, to visit for about an hour, and then return to Utah and the MTC. The members of my ward sacrificed financially to pay for the trip. I was so excited, I could hardly wait! My room was empty and quiet when everyone left to meet Paul at the airport. My mind reflected on all of the experiences we had shared together over the years. Now we could share this experience as well, even if for only a few moments.

In my most painful hours, he was coming to visit me. Not to play, or fight, or wrestle, or laugh; he was coming to suffer with me, to cry with me, and to comfort me. When he walked into that hospital room, my heart ached to have him see me this way. The pain I felt was intense, yet I knew he was suffering with me. We spoke general words like, "You look good," and "So, how have you been?" The tension was thick. Finally, I asked the others to excuse us. We left the hospital and Paul took me outside in the sun. It was there that two brothers communicated heart to heart again.

I told Paul not to worry about me. I shared with him many of the great spiritual experiences I had already enjoyed. I asked him to always pray for me, but not to mourn for me. I told him I was happy. I told him how grateful I was for these difficult times. I shared with him my personal walk with the Lord. We both faced the beginning of a long struggle and fight for what was right in our lives. He faced an uncertain future in the missionfield that would prove to be his life's greatest struggle up to that moment. I was in the middle of experiences and circumstances that would test my character and my beliefs. We faced two separate mountains but they were cut from the same stone. And so, in the warmth of that early afternoon sun, we resolved to begin our ascent together with songs of praise on our lips.

Reflections by Dallas

As I've grown older, I've learned a lot about a great principle called service. There are a thousand kinds of service.

76

It comes in all sizes and shapes. When I'm feeling depressed, lonely, sad, resentful, or of little worth, the best remedy I've found is to put my hands to someone else's burden, making both our hearts light and happy. It became obvious in the hospital that Art understood that principle, too.

Since that first day in Las Vegas, I can never remember Art complaining or letting his frustrations out on others as a result of the things he was suffering. I never witnessed him showing resentment, bitterness, anger, or regret for any of the tragedies he experienced. Here I am—a person with a life of ease— struggling for patience, and yet Art, who had a hundred reasons for impatience every day, became my example and teacher.

A lot of our friends and loved ones came to offer comfort and hope to Art. As I sat in that room day after day, I saw something incredible happen over and over again. Our friends left with a heart more full of love for their Father in Heaven, and with a smile on their faces. I was amazed as I listened to Art quietly redirect conversations from his problems to the person who was visiting him. "Oh, I wish I could see your new puppy!" he'd exclaim, or, "How are you doing in school?" He was constantly wanting to know how the other person was. These friends seemed to feel better about themselves, and not so bad for Art when they left. Being around him helped all of us recognize our blessings and, ironically, Art's blessings, also.

The accident and pain Art suffered did not change who he was. He was just as committed to life as ever and exemplified enthusiasm and high spirits in everything he did. I don't believe he realized the impact he had on others. I saw their faces and the expressions in their eyes. So many times, while visiting sick or injured people, we feel depressed or saddened and we take those feelings with us. But Art would not be defeated by this accident or anything else that would happen to him, and people took that attitude away with them.

Sometimes, late at night, I would sit by his bed for hours and we would just talk. We would cry together, and it was at those times that I saw some of the hurt he felt. It wasn't that Art was perfect, it was just that he has a resiliency and a sturdiness about him that saw him through. I know the source of his strength, because he often made it clear. The Lord walked with him; He walked with me, too.

Time is . . .
Too slow for those who wait,
Too swift for those who fear,
Too long for those who grieve
Too short for those who rejoice;
But for those who love. . .
Time is Eternity!

— Henry Van Dyke —

Chapter Seven
My Greatest Gift

Together. That was the most appropriate word to describe where we wanted to be. For five years Dallas and I had laughed together, had fun together, experienced life together, and grown closer and closer to one another.

We never dreamed of being apart. When we shared our dreams, we talked about our forevers together. We spoke of happy times, children, and romance. To be together meant everything to us. It was our world. It seemed at times as though every dollar we made was being spent to fulfill that end. We were either talking long distance on the phone, sending cards and letters, or saving money to make trips back and forth to Utah and California. Our lives revolved around the idea of being together. And why? For all the best reasons. When we were together we felt happiest. Our hearts were light and our spirits soared. Together, our greatest ambitions, dreams, and righteous desires bubbled to the surface. Every moment together was a new thrill in discovery and understanding. It seemed that the more we were together, the more we wanted to stay that way forever.

Our strong feelings for one another smoothed the sharp edges from both of our personalities. Through our years of dating and discovery, we shared many experiences which resulted in exciting memories for both of us. Much of the time our personalities floated gently and agreeably down the rivers of life together, but, at other, more difficult times, they bumped each other again and again as we experienced trying circumstances. Through it all, we learned of each other, understood each other's needs with increasing intimacy, and became more committed to each other's happiness. We were in the daily process of "falling in love."

After the accident, we found ourselves thrown together into what would seem a nightmare that neither of us had anticipated. The weeks before a wedding date traditionally bring happy times together. These should have been moments one remembers with a broad smile for years to come, not with a face twisted with pain and pillows soaked with tears.

Someone has said that, "the same winds snuff out candles, yet kindle fires; so where adversity kills a little love, it fans a great one." The cold winds of pain and struggle were blowing relentlessly in our lives. An instantaneous miracle in the beginning could have sheltered us from the harsh influence of that storm, but what would we have given up? As the winds blew day after day, Dallas and I enjoyed the benefits of more enriched communication and heightened feelings. Our dreams became more solidified, our perspective widened, our understanding deepened, our tolerance enhanced, and our commitment strengthened. During one short struggling period of time, we learned what a thousand hours of marriage seminars could not teach. I call that a miracle.

Surely we were disappointed at the unexpected delay of our plans for sealing our love in the temple, but we also knew that our love could not be denied forever. Time would eventually yield herself to unconditional love, and our day would come.

Reflections by Dallas

The time had come for my parents and I to return home from Las Vegas, so I could settle some affairs before heading to California where Art would be going in a few days. I wanted to spend every second with him, not wanting to miss a moment in his life. When it came time for me to say goodbye, I bent down close to Art while sitting on the bed and slipped my arms beneath his back. I wanted so much to be close to him, even in this awkward state. Although he was too weak to raise his arms, I felt his love and warmth as my tears moistened both our cheeks. "I hate goodbyes," I whispered. I made a bright, cheerful sign and pinned it up on the ceiling so Art could see it. He smiled warmly, showing his appreciation and acceptance. On the sign I had written, "I have happy toes." I told him to look at it often and envision his toes being alive and happy. Forcing myself from his side, I packed the few belongings I had brought with me and loaded them into the car. Most of my nights had been sleepless while in Las Vegas, and, as my parents and I started our eight hour drive home, I fell into an exhausted slumber.

When we arrived home, everything that had been going on before I had left, now seemed insignificant. Most of my impending wedding plans had been cancelled, but that day I received a call. My wedding dress was in. Would I like to see it? With labored hesitancy, I told the manager, who was a friend of mine, about the circumstances of the past ten days. She was saddened and said she would store the dress until I needed it. Most of the people I was close to knew of our marriage plans. I had excitedly shared the news as only a bride-to-be could. Now I had to explain our change of plans to everyone I saw.

After being home for several days, I became very depressed, which is unusual for me. A barrage of conflicting positive and negative thoughts crowded my mind and I felt confused. At first I could not determine what was causing the feelings. God had told us through his priesthood that Art would recover fully, according to his will. However, a question continually came up in my mind. Could I accept the Lord's will even if he didn't heal Art?

Even today, we know that when Art has accomplished his mission, he will be healed. I believe this with all of my heart. However, I think my Father in Heaven wanted to know if I could accept my circumstances even if the terms were significantly different. The thought echoed: "If the Lord's voice had been silent regarding our desires, if Art really wasn't going to be healed, how would I react then?"

I struggled with this question for three days and was emotionally and spiritually in pain. However, as my feelings became clearer and clearer, and knowing that I could not lie to God, I finally came to my heartfelt, honest answer. My struggle brought new understanding and an endowment of faith; I felt a great sense of joy that far outweighed the discouragement. If Father said no, and Art was to remain in a wheelchair for the rest of his life, I could still accept the Lord's perfect and flawless plan for us.

The day before I was to leave for California, I was walking through the mall with my sister and saw an old friend. She knew about my wedding plans and asked a question I'd heard quite often throughout that week. "Are you excited?"

"Yes," I told her, but added that my plans had been delayed. I explained that Art had been in a serious automobile accident and had broken his neck.

"Does that mean he is in a wheelchair?" she asked

"Yes, that was the prognosis, but I know he won't be in it forever."

With a puzzled look on her face she asked, "Well, I'm sure you're not going to marry him still—are you? I mean, how could you—with the way things are now?"

Her question took me completely off guard. For a moment, I wasn't sure whether to take her seriously. But, she was dead serious, and, as I looked her straight in the eyes, I tried to convey to her that I could not imagine life without Art, and that I felt very blessed to still have him. The uncomfortable silence that followed revealed that she didn't understand real love at the time, although I suspect she would now that she has a wonderful husband and two children. She would undoubtedly feel as I did if something ever happened to one of them.

I spent the rest of the day thinking about that question and analyzing the shock I felt at the new thought. Call me naive, but there was never a question in my mind as to whether I would still marry Art. I knew with all my heart that it was the right thing. Even beyond that, it was the good thing.

I had never had the thought enter my mind that I *wouldn't* marry Art. I shared the experience with Art on the phone that night. Quietly, he said, "I never asked myself that question either." He knew I would come to him and that I would stay forever. After all, we loved each other. We wanted to be together—for eternity.

———————————

Perhaps, for some, the feelings we have just shared are difficult to understand. Others may smile warmly and nod their heads as they relate to our situation. Behind every romance is often an inspirational story or two. It's important to know, however, that our strong feelings evolved over a long period.

Our decision to be together forever had been made many months before, even though the events of the accident overshadowed the circumstances of that choice.

Our feelings had not always been as we have described them, although they were continually growing in that direction. However, one experience seemed to cement our hearts together. From that moment, we knew we belonged together.

The setting was the spectacular Olympic Mountains in Washington. I had been working in Port Angeles and Seattle during the summer months, selling educational materials to families. The beauty of Washington and the Olympic Mountains needs to be shared. I invited Dallas to come and spend a few days with me. So, as in the years past, she loaded her car and made the drive from Utah to Washington to be with me.

Definitely committed more to Dallas than to my job of selling, I retired my demo-case for the next few days and we explored the splendors of Washington together. We spiraled our way to the top of the Space Needle in Seattle. We visited the newly constructed temple grounds. We rode on the ferries from one point of interest to another. We pedaled a "bicycle built-for-two" around a beautiful park. We took a cruise from a Seattle port to see the colorful flowers of Victoria on Vancouver Island, Canada. We raced from one end of Washington to the other trying to experience it all together.

July 15th was Dallas's birthday. I wanted it to be special and different, an experience to remember. As it turned out, I seriously doubt if it will ever be forgotten.

We were in the Port Angeles area at the time, nestled at the base of the Olympic Mountains. A short drive from the city, yet high in the tops of the Olympics, is a deep blue, glacier lake called Lake Crescent. This was the place I wanted to share with Dallas on her birthday.

It was a quiet lake with few tourists. I packed a nice picnic lunch, complete with a flower, blankets, and iced cookies with raisins—my favorites! It was a perfect day—the sun was shining and there was a light breeze. We slowly pushed the canoe from the dock after a few brief words of caution from the rental manager. "Stay out of the water, folks. It's awful cold in there. It's made for lookin' at and fishin' in—not for swimmin'. Glacier water, ya' know. A man could freeze in there before too long." We smiled our understanding and softly glided out onto the lake.

We paddled out before eating the picnic lunch. We laughed and talked as we always did. After we finished eating, we exchanged small talk about the different cloud shapes. Then, in a more serious vein, for the first time we talked about getting married. We shared open and honest feelings, and felt so close as we held each other and forgot the world. However, while forgetting the world, our canoe had drifted around the bend of the lake. It was a large lake, so we were quite a distance from the docks and any other people. The sun was setting, and we thought we'd better hurriedly paddle back before dark.

As we glided through the glass-covered water, we couldn't repress ourselves. Gently and playfully we splashed one another. Before long, our small splashes became a full-scale effort to completely soak each other. Then came the mistake. She leaned in one direction to splash the water with as much force as she could muster. I, too, leaned to avoid the splash. The problem was we both leaned the same direction. Almost in slow motion, the canoe rolled on its side and spilled us and our belongings into the icy cold waters of Lake Crescent. We looked at each other in shock as the words of the rental manager echoed in our minds: "Stay out of the water, folks. Glacier water, ya' know. A man could freeze in there before too long."

Instantly, we were soaked to the skin, and felt as though we had been thrown into a tub filled with ice. Our joints reacted quickly and became stiff and slow in their movements, making turning the canoe back over an impossible task. At the expense of a great deal of energy, however, we were able to lift our upper bodies from the water by draping ourselves across the bottom of the canoe.

Our predicament was obvious. We were far from shore. Even the strongest of swimmers would have struggled, not mentioning the fact that the freezing cold water would have completely worn them out long before they reached their destination. No one was to be seen anywhere on the shore, and with dusk casting its long shadows, we would be almost impossible to detect, anyway. Our upper bodies pulled out of the freezing waters definitely bought us some time, but the mountain winds were now blowing stronger through the rocky canyon. The wind sent chills through our bodies as it cut through our wet clothes. Somehow, this was not the birthday surprise I had planned.

Our eyes searched the distant shore again and again, hoping to see someone who could save us. As we continued to search, our faith began to dim. We had managed to hold onto one life jacket. The other had drifted aimlessly away while we were struggling with the canoe. I handed the life jacket to Dallas and asked her to put it on. Her eyes began to water as she softly shook her head back and forth. We looked into each other's eyes and in that moment we each clearly saw into each other's hearts. Neither of us wanted to take the life jacket. When we were together, life was fun, happy, and meaningful. The thought of not being together terrified us. In those few moments our hearts became one. For the first time, the life of someone else was infinitely more important to each of us than our own. We had to be together. We *would* be together.

"Can we have prayer?" Dallas's words echoed my feelings. Softly we held hands across the canoe and pulled our heads close to help keep us from shaking so violently. Our bodies had become numb from the icy waters. Our breathing was heavy and labored. Hope was fleeing as the light of day faded. And then we prayed. "Our Eternal Father in Heaven. We, thy children, come humbly before thee in prayer, in our desperate hour of need. We are alone and cold, and don't know what to do. Now, we ask thee, we plead with thee for our very lives. Send a savior to us to rescue us from these waters. We thank thee for hearing us. In the name of Jesus Christ we pray. Amen." To many, the odds would still have seemed long, but our hearts instantly felt peaceful.

Again, our eyes searched the distant shores—only this time we picked up the movement of someone walking along through the trees. We yelled loudly for help. The person stopped and looked—straining to see where the shouts were coming from. I grabbed one of the canoe paddles we had salvaged, put the orange life jacket atop it, and raised it high above the water. Now he saw us.

Calling for help, he ran to the water's edge and jumped into a row boat. He grabbed the oars, began to row, and his boat slowly moved forward. We watched for a moment, and then weakly chuckled. The man was drunk. He kept weaving all over the lake in his efforts to get to us! Fortunately, the other people he had alerted were in another rowboat, and reached us before our friendly drunk did.

As we were pulled from the water, it was almost impossible for us to move. We shook violently as our rescuers wrapped warm blankets around us. In a few moments, a ranger's speedboat pulled alongside and raced us to a warm cabin with a glowing fire where we could dry off and relate our adventure.

Because of that experience, we learned of our deep love for one another. We knew that somehow and someday, our love would lead us to the temple for an eternal sealing. We also knew that if we had not been living our lives in such a way that we felt clean and worthy, we may have never had the faith to cry those desperate words to our Father that day.

Now, because of my accident, our lives were intertwined into a different "Lake Crescent," only the solution wasn't so immediate. But our hearts were one, and they could not be separated now. Following her short leave in Utah to settle her affairs, Dallas was back by my side again in the hospital in California. Every day she stayed with me, helped me, encouraged me, and pushed me on. She made every sacrifice to be there with me. She moved permanently from her family and friends in Utah to California, a place often unfriendly and threatening to newcomers. She took a job in a place where she could be near the hospital, and she lived in church members' homes close by. Void of her usual crowd of friends and associates, she made my bedside her home and her night life was in the dim and smelly halls of the hospital.

Reflections by Dallas

I felt strange as I headed for California. I was leaving my familiar mountain home, my loving family and friends, and I felt unsure of what my future held. While it was a permanent move, it was so different from what I had planned. I would be spending my days in a hospital and my nights alone in a new city filled with over a million people—a frightening and confusing place. Never had I missed my home and family more than I did for the next eighteen months as I stayed in twelve different homes. These great people, my host families, were very supportive and gracious as they shared their homes and resources with me, but at times, I still felt so lonely. The only time I felt secure was when I was with Art. He brought so much happiness to me, even in his weakened condition. We would wait for the quiet hours of the evening, and then, getting as close as we could to each other (the halo brace made it almost impossible to even hug Art) we would pour out our hearts to one another. We shed a lot of tears during those late hours as we shared our new dreams and hopes and grateful feelings for our Savior. We were always so astounded at the blessings he gave to us.

I found myself leaving the hospital later and later each night, not wanting to leave my only source of comfort and security. On one particular night, I left at about 2:00 a.m. Trying to make my way back to Hollister (an hour and a half away) I got lost. That night my loneliness peaked until I thought I couldn't stand it anymore. I've never felt so alone. I was scared in that unfamiliar place and needed comfort desperately. With tears blurring my vision, I poured out my heart in prayer to a Father I knew was listening. "Dear Father, please let me know thou art near. Please grant me thy peace and understanding. I feel thy hand in the trials and adversities that lie in my path, but I need help. Could thou please send me thy love?" Tears flow, even now, as I recall the feeling that enveloped me. It was the most real, warm, and peaceful feeling I had ever experienced. I felt like a baby being held in the most loving arms imaginable. A divine presence permeated my soul with love. I felt understood, loved, and at peace. After that night, I never had those painful, lonely feelings again.

This same unseen presence has often been with me to lend an invisible, loving hand. For a year, until we got a van, I would lift Art's wheelchair into the back of our trunk and it was very heavy for me. Once when it was raining, the hatchback on our car wouldn't stay open, and my right arm was almost useless because of an injury. I also happened to be wearing a white dress! I stood under the heavy clouds, crying tears of frustration as I wondered how I was to hold the umbrella, hold up the hatchback, and lift the chair in, all with one arm. I realized I would have to put the umbrella down. I held the hatchback open and reached to lift the wheelchair with my injured arm. Suddenly, I felt invisible hands lifting also. The chair felt light as a feather—as did my burden. The chair slid into the trunk with no effort at all. Now, my tears were of gratitude—a small but significant miracle had taken place.

I praise God each day for his incredible love and mercy toward me and for easing my aching soul. I can't read the story of "Footprints in the Sand" without tears, for that story has come to life for me as my Lord countless times has carried me in his perfect arms and healed my broken heart.

I often found myself hoping that the plans Art and I had made would still materialize; when February 1st rolled around, maybe we could still be married. It was hard to face the reality that we'd have to start our plans all over again. Those plans were special to us, they were ours, they were personal and we'd thrown our hearts into them. As the weeks slipped by, deep down I knew we couldn't be married in February. It was a gradual process; however, once I had changed my thinking, I looked forward to making new plans with the same fervor as I had making the old ones.

Being an eternal optimist, I knew that in some way I could

still make February 1st a special day. The hospital food sometimes left a lot to be desired. The Mexican food tasted like the meatloaf; the meatloaf tasted like the stew; the stew tasted like the pot roast; and the pot roast tasted like the Mexican food. It was one eternal round. I knew some good food would make Art happy. His favorite is steak and lobster, and so I arranged to buy two dinners with the "works" from our favorite local restaurant called Hungry Hunter. They don't normally have take-out, but after explaining the situation to them, they graciously prepared a wonderful meal and packed it for me. I borrowed some china and stemware from the family I was staying with and set up a formal candlelight dinner to surprise Art. He was so excited as I pushed the hospital gurney in, candles lit, and the smell of "real food" permeating the stuffiness of the hospital room. I pulled the hospital curtain around to provide what privacy was possible in a place where the lights never went out and you were always in the center of activity.

Art has an incredible way of looking at me that seems to pierce my very heart. He is loving in his mannerisms, so when we were settled in and I had a chance to catch my breath, Art responded with that very look. It had been a hard day for us. At 10:00 that morning our thoughts were far away in a beautiful temple, where in our imaginations we knelt at a sacred altar and were married. Tonight was to have been our wedding reception, and to be so far away from our dreams brought bitter-sweet feelings. But those feelings included a knowledge that our day would come. Art would get better and be able to leave the hospital. We would continue our lives and fulfill our dreams. In the meantime, the taste of steak and fresh lobster brought us quickly back to the experiences of the moment and we gave thanks for what we *did* have.

At the age of ninety-two,
Chauncey Depew was
asked the question: "What
is the most beautiful word
in the English language?"
in the English language?"
He quickly replied:
"Home."

Chapter Eight
Yellow Ribbons

The pressure began to build in my head. I shut my eyes tightly against the pain. My head jerked sharply a couple of times as the doctor leaned into his work. Finally, the bolt which held my halo brace firmly in place against my head, jarred loose. The sound of bone against metal echoed in my ears. Slowly, the four bolts which held me bound were removed. Alcohol was applied to the open wounds. (The scars left today serve as a reminder of my personal prison.) The pressure was now diminishing, and my head began to feel light. But I didn't mind. At last, I was free! My halo brace had been removed after twelve long weeks.

At first I was required to wear a neck brace to keep my head steady while my neck muscles learned to do their job again. It felt different to be able to move my neck at all after so long. I could turn and see things and look up and down. The end of the halo marked a new beginning for me. In just two short weeks, it would be time to go home.

The next fourteen days could not have traveled fast enough. Friday the 13th was to be my official release date. An unlucky day for some, but for me a whole new beginning. I felt like I was being "born-again."

There can be many "births" in any one life, all marked by new beginnings, significant choices, fresh opportunities, challenging decisions, and departures onto new roads of growth. Every "birth" brings with it new vision and perspectives. From these elements can come the ingredients miracles are made of. New perspectives and fresh beginnings precipitate change. And change, as we have discussed before, can be the greatest miracle of all.

The Apostle Paul wrote, "For now we see through a glass, darkly . . . ." (1 Cor. 13:12.) We see life through the glasses of our own experience. To dramatically change the experience is like being fitted with a new set of glasses. Things once dark, now are illuminated through our new perspective. Major corporations throughout the business world pay millions of dollars to get fresh perspectives and new vantage points to assist the direction of their companies. The individual experience of daily struggle, pain, and hardship provides opportunity for the miracle of perspective, vision, and new beginnings which assists us in seeing through new glasses, less darkly. Such was my experience. Soon I would be heading home, born-again and fitted with a new set of glasses. The world was fresh and new.

Before that time, however, many questions had to be answered. Choices made now would have a lasting impact on my future. As I prepared to leave the hospital, plans were being made regarding what kind of wheelchair I would need. It seemed evident to my therapist and doctor that an electric wheelchair was a necessity. Throughout my stay in the hospital, they had me using a heavy and cumbersome Everest-Jennings manual chair, the kind most people identify with. It's largely chrome, and weighs about 65 pounds. I felt clumsy and awkward in it. Maneuvering that big Everest-Jennings was difficult and tiresome, at best, but with the struggle came added strength and resolve. Each labored push produced a greater will to achieve and overcome.

More recently, there had been a flood of new chairs coming into the marketplace described as ultra-light and modern. That was what I needed. I had a fear of the electric wheelchair. I feared that if I got used to the ease and convenience of just pushing a button for my desires that my strength, enthusiasm and esteem would slowly deteriorate.

Now came the problem of convincing the staff. When I first mentioned my feelings, they resisted strongly, concerned for my new future. "You must use an electric wheelchair, Art. To get around this hospital on smooth linoleum floors is one thing, but for you to challenge the world without the use of a motor is not very feasible. You'll need an electrically powered chair."

"You don't understand," I replied. "I do not want an electric wheelchair. I won't use it. I want a manual chair." Finally, they consented to consider my proposal if I could pass a test of my strength and ability. On the first floor of the hospital, a track had been laid out measuring one-eighth of a mile. If I could push that distance in less than 30 minutes, I could have my manual wheelchair.

Dallas pushed me around the track the first time to give me a feel for what I had to do. There were few obstacles, just distance, so I felt confident I could meet the challenge. With stop watches set, the therapist enthusiastically yelled, "Go!" Slowly, I crawled off the starting line. I was on my way.

The first long hallway was a breeze. With Dallas walking at my side encouraging me, I felt that the rest of the track would be easily accomplished in the desired time limit. Rounding the first corner into the second long corridor I felt the first real signs of fatigue. My arms felt like lead and my shoulders were sore. My slow pace slipped to less than a crawl. Each push seemed to take increasing amounts of energy and effort. I couldn't believe it. I had most of the distance left to go and already I was exhausted.

Biting my lower lip, I silently prayed, "Please, Lord. Help me finish this. Lend me strength." I pushed on. My arms still felt like lead. My shoulders still ached. But, somehow, I managed to keep pushing. I rounded the second corner, and then the third. Completing the fourth corner, my final objective was in view—the finish line.

I could see the therapist smiling as I struggled to act as though I wasn't tired at all. I lifted my head and smoothly pushed across the line. The official time: 28 minutes. I got my manual wheelchair, and now I was ready to go home.

Going home would mean leaving the constant attention and care of a full staff of nurses and attendants. Although that thought thrilled me, it also meant that someone else would need to help me at home until time and strength allowed me to become more independent. In the hospital, even though some of my individual identity was lost, still my care was routinely performed. Who would help me now?

My family bravely and compassionately stepped forward to answer the need. With their desire to be of service would also come a personal price to pay in effort. Learning what it would require to adequately care for my personal needs meant that my father would have to leave his warm bed in Hollister at 4:15 every other morning for two weeks before my release and drive an hour's distance to the hospital to receive special training in the care of a quadriplegic. It also meant my family, particularly my mother and father, would have to schedule their days around my needs.

Great blessings have come into my life, which may have never been possible otherwise, because of my family's help and assistance. I saw them with new eyes and experienced their love through unique circumstances. I have become much closer to both my mother and father. They have become my friends. That is significant to me, because during my growing years when I was often struggling and fighting against everything that should have been important to me, my relationship with my folks suffered. Those are hard years to earn back. I was given another chance to develop a closer bond of appreciation with those I love. I call that a miracle, too.

Even though I don't need their assistance now as I did then, I humbly thank God for those golden opportunities. I could not have bought those experiences with all the money in the world. There always is a silver lining behind the dark clouds of misfortune, and more often than not, a gold one, too.

The thirteenth of April arrived—my lucky day. My collection of books, cards, dried flowers, and balloons were put into boxes. I slowly traveled the hallways and said my goodbyes to doctors, nurses, and other patients.

The inside of our small car was loaded to the ceiling with books and boxes as we pulled away from the hospital into the busy street. I was on the outside now. Only memories and physical scars remained to remind me of my hospital days. I was happy to be returning to my home.

Even though my four-month stay in the hospitals seemed an eternity to me, many others with similar injuries would be staying months longer. One gentle man I knew was hospitalized for more than a year before he was well enough to return home to his family and friends. While still enjoying the benefits of extended time under the conditions of pain, truly, the Lord had blessed me with a speedy recovery, returning me to my home and a new beginning.

Now I looked longingly out of the car window. We were passing from my childhood city of San Jose toward the green hills of Hollister where my family now resided. I found my mind drifting into an unknown future. How would I be accepted? What would I do now? Every scene that passed by my window looked so different now. Where once I saw streets, stop-lights, and people, now I focused on curbs, obstacles, ramps, and friendly faces within a crowd who might be willing to lend a helping hand when I needed it. Outside the care and protection of the hospital, my life was my own again. What I would become was up to me. I had a lot to think about.

Reflections by Dallas

The welcoming Hollister countryside was fragrant and green and the slight breeze cooled the air perfectly. It was exhilarating and exciting! Art's family and I had planned a surprise welcome home party for Art. As we made the drive toward Art's home, I wasn't too familiar with the green hills and rolling countryside Art had grown up in, so he became my tour guide, pointing out places he'd been hiking or motorcycle riding. As we talked about our dreams and goals, it all seemed so different and real. Life wasn't being lived in a bottle anymore. This was the real world with no more conceptualizing and talking in terms of theories. This was a new reality, and all our future hinged on it. Everything looked so new and challenging.

As we came closer to home, I watched Art's face as he saw the huge banner across the front of his house, complete with balloons and streamers. The trees and bushes all over the yard cast a yellow glow since they had all been filled with little yellow ribbons. I saw the tears well up in Art's eyes as friends and family members came to the curb to give their special welcome. It seemed that the whole ward had come! They had prayed for him, fasted for him, and cried for him, and now they wanted to welcome him home. The outpouring of love for Art was unbelievable and I thought of the inscription: "No man has failed who has friends."

A big potluck lunch was served in the backyard. We ate and laughed and talked about our yesterdays and tomorrows. We felt alive and loved.

As we finished the food, some of the family and guests gathered to play a wild game of croquet. It had been years since either Art or I had enjoyed that game. This was a chance for him to begin his journey back into his new world, complete with new opportunities and insights. When he tried to hold a mallet in his hands, his grasp was too weak to hit anything besides himself! With a little creativity, we figured out the most advantageous means for him to be able to play. Art watched, with some courage and a good sense of humor, as we secured the mallet to his forearm with sticky tape. Now he was armed and dangerous! We wheeled him around the yard, and with just the right angle, he'd swing the mallet with as much force as he could. Sometimes he made his mark, but mostly he hit the grass, his wheelchair, or someone else. With our familiar laughter ringing in his ears, he genuinely expressed, "It's great to be back home!"

Home never looked so good. The fresh smells of the country had never been more gratefully received. As I was helped from the car, I saw the long sloping ramp extending from the door of the house. As I was given a tour of our home, I saw signs of personal sacrifice and desires to help me in my new life. My brother had given up his ground-floor bedroom for my convenience. I felt like a blind man who had just received his sight, or a child who sees everything as new. My world looked so different than it had before. Immediately, I noticed the simple things, such as the height of door knobs, cabinet shelves, clothes rods in the closets, light switches, desks and tables. I noticed the width of hallways, door frames, and shower stalls; *and* the problem of stairs. I had a new set of challenges but with every challenge comes opportunity.

As soon as I was free to move around the house on my own, familiar words echoed in my ears, "You must use an electric wheelchair, Art. To get around this hospital on smooth linoleum floors is one thing, but for you to challenge the world without the use of a motor is not very feasible. You'll need an electrically powered chair." We had a plush carpet throughout much of our home. It was soft to the feet, but in the wheelchair it felt like I was pushing through sand. Every push required a great deal of energy and effort. Often, I could only push an inch or two before requiring some rest. It took me half an hour or more to get from one end of the hallway to the other. But I wouldn't complain. I knew that, in time, my strength would return. Effort *always* precipitates growth.

Before long I got used to being at home with my family and friends, and I settled into my new life. The learning process had just begun. One of my first big goals had been to get down the ramp in the backyard without requiring help. Because of the restrictions of space, it was a short, rather steep, ramp which led directly into a flower bed and tree. Each day I had my little brother, Roger, pull back on the wheelchair as I went down the ramp. As he would resist gravity, I would strain to help keep the chair at a controllable speed. Each day Roger complimented me on my improvement. Finally, one day I thought I could do it by myself. Being a cautious person, I did ask Roger to walk behind me and help *only* if I was getting out of control and really needed it. He agreed.

Having sympathy for my determination, yet knowing there was no way I could do it on my own, he helped all the way. When I got to the bottom, I eagerly asked Roger if he had helped at all. Wanting me to feel a sense of accomplishment, he told me proudly that he hadn't helped at all. I had done it on my own. I swelled with a false sense of achievement.

The next morning I eagerly asked my mother to come see the great thing I had learned. I knew she'd be proud. Asking her to stand at the bottom of the steep ramp, I told her I was going to demonstrate how I could get down by myself.

"Are you sure you can do this, Art?" she cautiously asked.

"Absolutely," I confidently replied. "Besides, I had Roger standing behind me yesterday in case I needed help, and I didn't need him at all. Just stand there and watch me go." I slowly pushed off. Instantly gravity took over and I began gaining momentum. I was shocked at the amount of speed I picked up so quickly. I held harder against the hand rims. I still went faster. Almost as quickly as I had begun, I was at the bottom, racing toward my mother, who now had a look of terror in her eyes.

"Stop me, Mom!" I yelled. She reached forward to try and slow me down. Too late. I hit her just below the knees at full speed, sending both of us flying into the flowers and tree.

"I thought you said you had it all under control!" Mother exclaimed.

"I did. Yesterday, Roger said . . . ." I thought for a moment, then both of us went to find Roger. We all had a good laugh, even though it was mostly at my expense. While neither of us had been hurt, we learned that a painful truth can sometimes be better than a kind lie! Later, I would learn to master that ramp on my own.

Everything that had once been old and routine was now new, exciting, and savored. Perhaps the sweetest experience came the first Sunday I was able to go to church again after sixteen long weeks of absence. The Sabbath day had been a meaningful part of my life before my accident, and I was anxious to return. I missed that association and spiritual renewal more than anything else.

I was a little nervous as I prepared to go to church. I was dressed in my Sunday best, and my wheelchair was polished to a brilliant sheen. Having not worn my church clothes at all during those weeks in the hospital, I noticed right away how much weight I had lost. My clothes hung on me. At first I felt self-conscious about how I looked and I hesitated. Then, in a moment, my new glasses brought a brighter focus into my view. I wasn't going to be in a fashion show. I was going to pay my devotions to my God; no matter how I looked, my heart and mind were prepared to come boldly before his throne.

It had been over four months since that fateful day I broke my neck and priesthood hands were laid on my head and a promise given that my legs would be all right and that I would walk again. By now, many had forgotten about that significant blessing and other similar blessings, but that thought was still in the front of my mind. Someday that blessing would become a reality. Until that time, I would wait and pray and prepare myself, but I would never forget.

"You won't be needing this belt will you, Art?" my father asked as we prepared for church. "After all, it's not likely you will lose your pants while sitting down," he chuckled.

Smiling, I asked, "But, what if I walk today, Dad? My pants are loose enough that I'm afraid I would shock folks more from my pants falling down in church than I would by walking." He laughed his acknowledgement, and slipped a belt on me, tightening it snugly.

When we got to church, we quietly slipped into the chapel. As we came through the door, members turned their heads and smiled in acknowledgement. We sat along the back row so we wouldn't block the aisle. Everything looked and felt so different. I was touched by the sincerity of the prayers, felt the reverence of the music, and the children—although sometimes restless—seemed so acceptable in this place of worship. I looked around me and instead of seeing common people living ordinary lives, I saw brothers and sisters excelling in their attempts to become disciples of Christ.

Soon, the congregation joined in singing the sacrament hymn. Tears quickly flooded my eyes as I sang the words, "I stand all amazed at the love Jesus offers me." Still feeling the adverse effects of my limited lung capacity, I had to stop occasionally for a deep breath. The quality of my singing could not adequately express the gratitude in my heart. As my hands reached for the emblems of our Lord's sacrifice, I fumbled with my uncoordinated, numb hands to grasp the soft bread. My limitations did not diminish the significance of renewing my baptismal covenants or the peace I felt. I had been given much for which to praise my Father in Heaven and his Eternal Son. By again humbly taking upon myself his name, I was, in limited measure, giving expression to my rejoicing.

Talks that once would have seemed slow and dry to me I now recognized as meaningful and sincere, and I hung on each word as it was expressed. Each talk, each hymn of praise, each prayer, made a personal and lasting impression. I felt like a convert to the Church experiencing everything for the first time.

For a special number, a sister began to sing, "I wonder when he comes again, will herald angels sing? Will earth be white with drifted snow, or will the world know Spring?" As she sang, my heart also sang. As the words of the song asked questions regarding the future of a glorious second coming, my mind pondered my new future. What would it hold for me? How could I make the best of a temporary, but difficult trial? Could I withstand the refiner's fire and transform my worthless dross into precious gold?

"I wonder if one star will shine, far brighter than the rest. Will daylight stay the whole night through, will songbirds leave their nests?" she sang with sincere devotion. With an overwhelming sense of peace and divine reassurance filling my heart and mind, my questions changed to thoughts of optimism and hope. The Lord would bless me as he had so many times before. Together, with his omnipotent power and influential love, all things would be possible. My mission president's words came into my mind: "A man cannot see his shadow if he is facing the sun. I don't know of anybody who has gone blind from looking at the bright side of things."

The song continued, "I'm sure he'll call his little ones together round his knee. Because he said in days gone by, 'Suffer them to come to me.'" Tears began to flow down my grateful cheeks. I left that meeting with an enormous feeling for the Lord's all-encompassing love for his children of all ages. I felt alive and loved. Never had a sacrament service been more meaningful or edifying. What had changed? The people? The bishop? The participants? Nothing had changed but the heart, vision, and perspective of someone who had been set on a new road.

The thoughts and feelings that came from that first sacrament meeting symbolized a new beginning for me. My whole world was different from what it had been during the months in the hospital. I was home; my life was mine. I felt like a child that was learning to crawl, then walk, and finally run. I was learning what I could do, what I couldn't do and what I hoped to eventually do—trying not to set limits on my growth. I was getting used to the new glasses; and people, objects, and the world around me became a new place of learning and understanding where nothing could be taken for granted anymore. The experience was something akin to this story as told by Frank Koch in *Proceedings*, the magazine of the Naval Institute:

Two battleships assigned to the training squadron had been at sea on maneuvers in heavy weather for several days. I was serving on the lead battleship and was on watch on the bridge as night fell. The visibility was poor with patchy fog, so the captain remained on the bridge keeping an eye on all activities.

Shortly after dark, the lookout on the wing of the bridge reported, "Light, bearing on the starboard bow."

"Is it steady or moving astern?" the captain called out.

Lookout replied, "Steady, captain," which meant we were on a dangerous collision course with that ship.

The captain then called to the signalman, "Signal that ship: We are on a collision course, advise you change course 20 degrees."

Back came the signal, "Advisable for you to change course 20 degrees."

The captain said, "Send, I'm a captain, change course 20 degrees."

"I'm a seaman second class," came the reply. "You had better change course 20 degrees."

By that time the captain was furious. He spat out, "Send,

I'm a battleship. Change course 20 degrees."

Back came the flashing light, "I'm a lighthouse."

We changed course.

(Stephen R. Covey, *Seven Habits of Highly Effective People*, 1989, Simon and Schuster, p. 33.)

I, too, had met with an obstacle I couldn't move. I changed my course.

One beautiful afternoon, Dallas and I were driving around running errands and enjoying each other's company. It wasn't long before it became necessary to fill the car with gas. As we pulled into the station and up to the self-service island, I felt distraught.

Typically, filling the car with gas was a function I would have performed for Dallas. Not only would it be the gentlemanly thing to do, but it was one of my personal ways of telling Dallas how much I loved and appreciated her. Now, due to the obvious change in circumstances, it became necessary for Dallas to do it.

Dallas, always able to understand my emotional pain, never uttered a begrudging word. She cheerfully jumped from the car and headed for the nearest gas pump, content with the knowledge that if I had been able to pump the gas, I would have gladly done it. As she began, another gentleman was servicing his own car. He watched Dallas for a moment as she worked. Then, with a curious look in his eyes, he glanced in my direction. He looked back at Dallas dutifully taking care of the needs of the car, then questioningly back again at me. His question was very evident by the look on his face. "Why is that beautiful girl filling the car with gas while that lazy man sits in the shade and waits? He looks well enough. What's his problem?"

Unwilling to put the question to rest in his mind, he approached Dallas. "Do you always fill the car? Why is that guy just sitting there while you do all the work? Who is he anyway, huh?"

Dallas's answer was simple and direct, "He's my fiancé and he's in a wheelchair." Dallas's response apparently took the man aback. He hung his head, embarrassed as he replied, "Oh. I'm sorry."

Dallas quickly continued, "He was hurt in a car accident a few months ago. He always did this job before, and he would do it now too, if he could. Thanks, though, for being concerned." Dallas walked back to the car.

As we drove off down the street, Dallas relayed the conversation that had taken place. That anguished feeling was there again, but I was glad the matter was cleared up. We talked about how easy it was for people to judge others. We discussed how "man only looks on the outward appearance, while the Lord looks on the heart." I felt relieved that the Lord would be my ultimate judge.

Just about the time we had sufficiently filled ourselves with an inflated sense of self-righteousness, we pulled into a food mart on the corner. We were thirsty and wanted to get something to drink. For obvious reasons, I stayed in the car as Dallas ran in to get our drinks. As I sat waiting, another car pulled into the stall beside me. Jumping from the car, a young lady went inside. A young man was with her, too, and I watched him from the corner of my eye. I watched the young lady pull two cold drinks from the refrigeration unit, pay for the drinks at the front counter and return to her car where the young man was waiting for his drink.

I couldn't believe my eyes. I was appalled that the young man would require the girl to go in after the drinks for *him*.

That was a job he should have cheerfully done himself. "He doesn't deserve a girl like that," I mentally criticized.

It was about then that I realized what I had just done. Immediately I let out a hearty laugh, this time at myself. Just minutes earlier I had given my mental reproach to the "unrighteous" judging of a man at the gas station who had honestly misjudged an innocent situation. Now, I laid that same judgment on someone else. Perhaps, the man was deserving of my mental assault. But, who was I to lay that charge to his name? I knew nothing of who he was, where he had come from, or what circumstances had brought him to where he now was. Surely, I did not understand the thoughts and intents of his heart, let alone have the insight and perspective necessary for a truly righteous judgement. Now, when I am tempted to lay a sin to anyone, for whatever reasons, I simply remember that day, and laugh.

I was learning what it meant to "Judge not, that ye be not judged." (Matt. 7:1.) Now at home, I had a host of resources to call on to help me learn many other things. Those resources included a supporting family, an affectionate sweetheart, faithful friends, and a loving Father in Heaven. I was prepared to begin my new life.

Two roads diverged in a yellow wood,
And sorry I could not travel both
And be one traveler, long I stood
And looked down one as far as I could
To where it bent in the undergrowth;

Then took the other, as just as fair,
And having perhaps the better claim,
because it was grassy and wanted wear;
Though as for that the passing there
Had worn them really about the same,

And both that morning equally lay
In leaves no step had trodden black.
Oh, I kept the first for another day!
Yet knowing how way leads on to way,
I doubted if I should ever come back.

I shall be telling this with a sigh
Somewhere ages and ages hence:
Two roads diverged in a wood, and I—
I took the one less traveled by,
And that has made all the difference.

— Robert Frost —

Chapter Nine
The Road Less Traveled

On June 18th, 1985, the sun was shining brighter and more beautifully than on any other day I can remember. The sky was deep, azure blue and the wind blew lightly, bringing fragrances of nearby flowers. Even if it had been the coldest, stormiest day of the year, my heart still would have glowed with the warm fire of dreams fulfilled.

We waited on the green lawns of the Salt Lake Temple for friends and family to gather. It had been almost two years since I had proposed to Dallas on a beach in Carmel, California. Now, our day had come. Our love would soon be sealed for all eternity. We never had to be apart again.

As we waited, my mind drifted back to a moment in time before the accident. I had been home from my mission for eight months. Many exciting changes were taking place in my life. I had temporarily postponed my plans for schooling for an opportunity to work with a master in the art of business. Together, we would start a tennis court construction and marketing company that would give me valuable, practical experience. My future looked exciting and bright.

There was just one major void in those plans. While starting a new business in California, I would be perpetuating the already wearisome distance between Dallas and myself. For almost five years we had dealt with this long distance romance.

Our love was true. Our friendship was firm. However, a more permanent relationship needed to be established.

I brought Dallas with me to California in August of that year under the guise of showing her the new business I was getting involved in. With an engagement ring burning a hole in my pocket, I was ready to officially ask Dallas to be my wife.

Parking near the ocean front of Carmel, a quaint, romantic town, I suggested, "Let's go down to the beach. It's a nice evening, we can go for a walk." Dallas softly agreed. This was the event I had dreamed of for years. I wanted the proposal to be special. I wanted it to be different. I wanted it to be romantic. What could be more romantic than a walk along a white-sand beach with the waves gently rolling in and the moonlight casting its reflection across the miles of water? It would be there, in the light of the glowing moon, that I would present that ring and ask the exciting question.

There was just one problem: as we trudged toward the beach through the thick sand, I noticed right away that it was rather dark. There was no moon out! However, I wouldn't let my plans be frustrated. I said, "Dallas, let's walk over there." Dallas had a confused look on her face, but reluctantly followed.

Standing next to a tree near the front entrance to the men's room, I was ready. The light was just right to present my proposal. (A little awkward, but at least there was light!) Standing Dallas squarely in front of me, and looking her in the eye, I asked, "Dallas, will you be my forever princess?" A half-smile came across her face, but she was still not registering exactly what I meant. Desiring to make my intentions clear I responded, "This is a proposal, just in case you're wondering."

A beautiful smile replaced the looks of confusion. She

beamed brightly and blushed. We held one another for a long time. Happy tears were shared as we dreamed together.

We never imagined how many tears would fall until the day we'd finally be married. Now, outside the walls of the temple, our months and years of dreaming were about to become a reality. The love I felt in my heart was unsurpassed by anything I had ever felt before in my life. In the weeks just past, as we talked through the details of weddings, such as picture-taking, receptions, and breakfasts, I could not erase the enormous smile from my face, nor from my heart. It was to be the happiest day of my life to that point. Many happier days have come, however, because of our decision together that night on the beach.

Dressed in white, I sat in the quiet beauty of the temple hallway waiting to enter the sealing room. As I wheeled myself in, I was overwhelmed by so many hopes and dreams being fulfilled. As I saw Dallas, clothed in the wedding dress that had waited so long for its bride, I fell in love with her all over again.

The temple sealer offered to let me remain in my wheelchair for the ceremony. However, I felt I *had* to kneel; it was a part of my dreams of a lifetime. My two brothers, holding me under my arms, gently lifted me from my chair, and helped me kneel at that altar. Holding Dallas's warm hand, I looked into her glowing eyes and smiled.

The words I only faintly recall today. But, the feeling—the feeling I will never forget. We both wept as the words of the ceremony were spoken. Our love was finally complete. If we had participated in the fairy tales of *Cinderella* or *Sleeping Beauty*, the joy and happiness could not have been more real and fulfilling than we were experiencing at that time. June 18th, 1985 was truly "our day."

Leaving the solace and peace of the temple, our new life

was beginning—together. A dream had been fulfilled. Now, fresh opportunities and challenges would come. So much had already been learned, but we were soon to learn more through the uniqueness of our circumstances.

In the weeks before we were married, we began the painstaking effort of finding a place to live. Before the accident, the task would have been much simpler, only now it was complicated by special considerations and needs. How many steps into the house? How wide were the doorways? How easy were the door knobs to turn considering my paralyzed hands? How much room in the bathrooms and shower? How open was the kitchen and how accessible the dish cabinets? The answer to each question was important to us.

Some of the obstacles could be overcome, such as building ramps for steps, while other needs were more difficult to adapt to. Some landlords were resistant to allowing any changes to be made to their property to accommodate my needs, while others seemed willing and considerate.

Following weeks of searching and asking questions, we found a small home to rent. My father and brothers built ramps, changed door knobs, lowered shelves, and widened doorways. "Home, sweet, home." Returning from our honeymoon, Dallas and I were ready to begin our new life together.

Living in California is expensive, regardless. However, when we added the expense of wheelchairs, doctors, and medical supplies, it became a financial burden requiring that both Dallas and I work full-time to meet our growing needs.

Despite our strong relationship prior to marriage, Dallas and I still had to learn greater communication skills. Our lives required a unique interdependency. I needed Dallas to help me with the many little things I still could not do for myself, while Dallas depended on me for emotional support, to do what things I could, and to be the priesthood leader in our home. Friction or debate with each other only compounded the difficulty of our circumstances. Quickly we learned how to enhance our listening and communication skills, as well as our ability to sincerely and quickly say, "I'm sorry."

It was difficult not being able to do the things typically required of a man in the home. I couldn't mow the lawn, fix the dripping faucet, change the oil in the car, or move the heavy furniture for cleaning. That's where friends and family came in to help.

What things I could do, I did. I picked things up around the house, even though it took me much longer than it would the average person. Sometimes I dragged the vacuum cleaner behind me around the carpet. I cleaned the kitchen, wiped the table, and loaded the dishwasher—only breaking a few dishes! And when I could, I fixed dinner.

I had learned, through necessity, how to get the things I needed in the kitchen and to prepare a simple meal. My first real experience began one long day after working without breakfast or lunch. Returning home in the late afternoon, I was famished. I was so hungry that I felt weak and light-headed. Dallas wouldn't be home from work for another hour, so I decided it was time to learn to fend for myself in the kitchen.

Our kitchen was small and not very accessible to wheelchairs. Maneuvering myself into place, I got the refrigerator door open. There were two slices of bread left—both heels—but I was starving, so I thought I'd make a sandwich.

In spite of limited use of my hands, I managed to get the mayonnaise, mustard, cheese, ham, and lettuce from the refrigerator without dropping or breaking anything. Working my way to the table with the food balanced on my lap, I laid out my workplace.

My first challenge was to get the jars open. Using teeth, towels, and hands, I finally opened the jars of mayonnaise and mustard. With a sharp knife I carefully sliced open the packages of ham and cheese. Now, with spatula in hand, I was ready to begin my construction work. Using both hands to grip the spatula, I tried spreading the mayonnaise on the bread, but the bread kept moving around the table. Positioning my bread between a couple of jars and on top of my towel, I tried again, successfully. I had learned a new trick! After spreading the mayonnaise and mustard, I carefully laid my cheese, ham, and lettuce on the slices of bread and brought them together— project completed, and after only forty minutes, too! I beamed with pride. This was a real accomplishment for me and I was anxious to taste my creation. My stomach growled impatiently.

As I eagerly raised the sandwich to my lips, the phone rang. Putting the sandwich down on the edge of the table, I pushed into the other room to answer the phone.

It was Dallas telling me she was leaving work to come home. Excitedly, I explained my new skill, giving step-by-step details of how I had accomplished the formidable task. Dallas proudly acknowledged my achievement. Hanging up the phone I returned to the table, anxious to satisfy my appetite. The sandwich was gone! As I quickly surveyed the room, I found my dog, mustard still on her whiskers, licking her chops.

A few weeks later, Dallas had to work overtime one evening. With my new skill, I decided to try something more challenging than a sandwich. Within a short time, I had prepared a steak and baked potato dinner, complete with a tossed green salad (the tossing part was the easiest!) and candles. By fixing a whole meal, I had added to my growing list of things I *could* do.

Reflections by Dallas

Our wedding had been like a dream for Art and me. I'm a very idealistic person and wanted and expected a "fairy tale" event. It was; so when a few months had gone by, I realized I would need to adjust to real life soon. I felt almost selfish, not wanting to give up the magic of our wedding. But I found that the special feeling didn't leave—it changed to a warm and soft security that wrapped around us as our love grew.

For some, the first year of a new marriage is the hardest. For Art and me it was easy. The hard time came with the second year. I had pneumonia and bronchitis. Art also had a bad case of bronchitis which is extremely difficult to recover from with his paralyzed chest muscles. I could hardly take care of myself, let alone Art, who was very weak and needed constant attention. While laying around the house not wanting to move or talk,we both worried about missing work. I was in a high stress job with long hours and I was feeling the pressure of not being there.

Frankly, I wanted my mom. I wanted to be babied and pampered. I wanted someone to take care of me. I was so sore from coughing that tears would come with each attack. I felt tired of taking care of others and felt there was no one for me. I would think back to the times when I was sick and my mom was there with juice and a back rub.

One night I was feeling particularly sorry for myself and was trying to clean up the kitchen. I had just emptied the dish washer and stacked the clean, new dishes in the cupboard when the top shelf collapsed. Each shelf fell on top of the other breaking glasses, plates and bowls. Some managed to come crashing down on me. So, there I stood amid the glass and mess with tears rolling down my cheeks. I was mad at anything and everything. I didn't have the strength, let alone the desire, to clean up the mess. For a moment I wanted a husband who could come and clean it up for me—one who would rescue me from my sorry state.

I went in our den and crashed on the floor and spent the next half-hour crying. I called my mom, my sister, and my best friend, wanting someone to feel sorry for me too. None of them were home. Feeling extremely alone, I finally called on Father in Heaven for help. I told him that he could have Art walk now because I was sure I was being tested beyond my ability to handle my situation. I wanted to believe that if I quit or gave up, the Lord would have to change things. Wouldn't that prove I couldn't endure any more?

I'm glad Father has a good sense of humor and that he loves us so much. After all I said and did, he still comforted me, and I was led to read in the Book of Mormon in Mosiah 21:3 where the people are in bondage to the Lamanites. They were being taxed and burdened heavily, and instead of asking for deliverance, they asked for the capacity to bear their burdens and to endure their trials or adversity. Still I did not want to bear *my* burden anymore or to admit that I could go on.

After some struggle over the next few months, I began to experience new tolerance and strength. I truly believe that the Lord grants us the things we need in order to continue on. Looking back, my former concerns seem trivial to me. I have come so far and the things that were hard for me then are easy for me now. Isn't that the Lord's way—to make weak things strong?

Over the past years since we've been married, I've gained an appreciation for what it means to have strong, constant support. Art may not be able to take out the garbage or fix my shelves, but the emotional and spiritual support he constantly lends, more than makes up for it. I don't care if my husband can't cut the lawn or change the oil in my car as long as he can listen to me and understand my heart. It is of greatest value to me to have a husband who has learned to be a patriarch and spiritual leader in the home.

Through the process of living with Art, I've learned to do many things around the house that I can take pride in. Art makes me feel like a million dollars—as if I can do anything. No one can put a price on someone who loves the Lord, who is forever patient, and who loves unconditionally. To have a husband who never puts me down or belittles me is priceless. I've quit looking at what I *don't* have and focused upon what I *have*. What a difference it has made!

And so we were living. Dallas and I were learning together and growing in our love and affection. We found new ways to serve each other, communicate, and adapt. Dallas loved me to go shopping with her—I make a great shopping cart! Less meaningful parts of living now became experiences essential to growth and development as well as enjoyment.

Not long ago, we were doing some shopping at a mall. Dallas had just a couple of items to get, so while she headed for the department store, I slipped into one of my favorite places—a bookstore. Since it was almost closing time, I told Dallas she could easily find me among the books when she was finished. She hurried off.

I spent the next few minutes searching through hundreds of interesting titles in the back of the store. Soon I heard Dallas's footsteps coming up the long aisle. From the months in the hospital, I had learned to recognize the sound of her distinct walk. Almost without thinking, I hid behind a bookshelf as she walked past. She hadn't seen me. This was going to be fun.

Reaching the back of the store and not finding me, she turned and started back. I hid again, this time in the mystery section. She walked past. Knowing that if I hid for too long it could make an unpleasant situation, I decided to give away my hiding place by whistling at her. Dallas and I often whistled sexily at one another as a show of affection. I whistled just loud enough for her to hear. The footsteps hesitated, stopped, and then began again toward the rear of the store. Not wanting to make this too easy, I slid behind another shelf of books as she walked right by. I chuckled to myself as I considered my advantage. With the hunt now well in progress, I whistled affectionately again, only this time louder. The footsteps began toward me, quicker than before. I slid behind a different set of shelves. She walked right past. This was *too* easy. It never took Dallas this long to figure out what I was doing. She was headed for the front of the store again.

This is ridiculous, I thought. I'd give her one last chance before I surrendered. I whistled that affectionate tune again, as loud as I could. The footsteps stopped, paused a moment, and then quickly continued. I was confused. I concluded that I should give myself up. I pulled into the open aisle, "Hi, sweetheart," I shouted, "I'm over here." The blond hair swung around—it wasn't Dallas!

My face turned about fifty different shades of red as the young woman manager replied, "I'm sorry, sir, but we're closing, and I couldn't find you." She blushed a little herself.

Tucking my chin under, I mumbled, "Thank you, I was leaving anyway." Dallas laughed when I told her.

With each experience I had, each new, little skill I learned, worlds of opportunity opened. Learning to drive again was one of my greatest breakthroughs. When I was in the hospital, I was told that I would never enjoy the privilege of driving again. For the first year after leaving the hospital, Dallas chauffeured me from place to place. She helped me into the passenger seat, folded my chair up, and loaded it into the back of the car. There was no such thing as "running in" anyplace. Everywhere we went required effort and time. Bad weather made getting places even more difficult.

Less than two years after my accident, this whole picture changed. My strength and abilities had improved to the point that we had a van built especially for my needs. When my new, converted van first pulled into my driveway, I could hardly contain my enthusiasm. It had a hydraulic lift on the side door to get me and my wheelchair in, a raised roof for my height, a driver seat that pivoted completely around so that I could climb into it, and hand-controls which operated the brake and accelerator. Riding the lift up for the first time, I felt like an eight-year-old boy on Christmas morning.

The real test came, however, when I had to transfer myself into the driver's seat. While I had developed enough strength during the last year to push myself successfully from place to place, lifting my 150-pound body was a different matter. Resisting offers for help, I struggled, groaned, and pushed, as I tried to lift my body out of the wheelchair and into that seat. Twenty minute later I was in the new seat and prepared to drive for the first time since my accident.

Learning to drive again with just my hands was a unique experience. It felt like playing a video game—only the other drivers on the road didn't think it was a game. Practicing in very large, *empty* parking lots, before long I was ready to brave the real world, and I have been "braving it" ever since. I soon learned to get into or out of my van in only three or four minutes. Today I drive a newer van which is built to accommodate me in my wheelchair so I don't have to transfer to another seat. Consequently I can get in and out of it as fast as anybody else could. A world of opportunity has opened to me.

I had been using my van for more than two years and enjoying every benefit it offered me when I learned that we don't fully appreciate something until we lose it. I commuted twenty-two miles each way to work. That kind of distance every day would be impossible for me to accomplish independently without my van—or so I thought until my van had a major engine problem which would require it to be in the shop for more than three weeks. Dallas worked every day too, and so depending on her to get me to work was out of the question. I needed to find a way to work independent of Dallas or my family. Problems, however, bring with them new perspective and opportunities for learning.

In California, some of our city busses have wheelchair lifts on them. Carefully mapping out the route I would have to take, I made my plans. Leaving for work two hours early, I pushed the half-mile to the first bus stop. As the bus pulled up, the driver operated the wheelchair lift. The doors opened, the steps flattened out into a platform, and lowered to curb height. As I rolled onto the platform, the driver again operated the controls and the platform raised into the bus. I rolled in, found my reserved space, and locked my wheels. The platform then collapsed back into the form of steps, the door shut, and the bus pulled away from the curb. We were off! Thirty minutes later, knuckles white from holding on for dear life, I got off the bus at my first transfer. Boarding the next bus, I took my final ride to work. At quitting time, the process began again for my return home.

What an experience! Everything worked smoothly—until one day. The bus pulled up to the curb and the driver began his routine of forming and lowering the platform. Rolling onto the platform, I began my ascent. Halfway to the top, the platform stopped. The driver played with the switches, but was unable to get the platform started again. All fifty passengers on the bus began to look at their watches, anxious to get to work on time. In a few minutes, the driver solemnly announced, "I'm sorry, folks, I will have to call for a repairman. Please get off the bus and wait for the next one." Passengers moaned and grumbled as they got off the bus. I don't know why they were complaining—I was the one still stuck on the platform! An hour later, the bus was fixed, and I was on my way again.

The next day as I boarded the same bus, the platform stopped again. The same fifty passengers nervously eyed the driver. In a few minutes, he made the same announcement. The passengers grumbled so loudly I thought I was going to be lynched! One passenger announced his idea to start a collection to get my van fixed sooner! Ten minutes later, another bus came along and all fifty passengers loaded into it. Coupled with the passengers already on board, most of the fifty were forced to stand for their thirty minute ride to work on a bus that stops at every bus stop. The bus on which I was stranded was an express bus which made only half the normal stops.

No sooner had the new bus pulled away from the curb than the driver of my bus got the platform to work again. Quickly, I rolled into my space, locked in, and the bus, with the driver and myself only, pulled into traffic. A few minutes later we passed the overcrowded bus. The driver, displaying his sense of humor, said, "Wave as we go by. I'll honk!" I found a new bus route the next day.

With all the learning, adapting, and new discoveries, I still never completely get used to the feeling of being paralyzed. While I have enjoyed the experience, opportunities, and learning which come from being in a wheelchair, it is often difficult and frustrating. Many things once so easy are now impossible. When simple obstacles stand in my way, I have to battle at times to keep from feeling trapped or claustrophobic. Simple things, such as steps, heavy doors, wind, narrow aisles, or crowds of people, can instantly turn my optimism and ability into discouragement. Staying at home, or shutting myself in my own world, would be the easiest answer, but would deny opportunity and change. To risk is to exercise faith; to risk frustration is to step onto the road which leads to miracles and opportunities—to risk in spite of difficulty is essential to growth.

Adversity for many is seen as a formidable obstacle on the road to their happiness and fulfillment. But struggle, pain, and despair are not obstacles so much as they are detours which seem to lead us *away* from our hopes, dreams, and righteous aspirations, but in reality can head us *toward* them. And while the way is stony, and requires a lot of risking, I have discovered that the panorama can be breathtakingly beautiful.

As a young boy scout on my first fifty-mile backpacking trip, I learned some valuable lessons about the roads of life. On the third day of hiking, we came to a point in the trail where a fast-moving river blocked our way, and getting around it meant hiking extra miles. To keep us on schedule, another trail was chosen, which had a 3500 foot climb in elevation over a short distance, taking us over the summit and back onto our designated trail.

Attempting to avoid the blistering heat of the day during the hardest parts of the climb, we began our climb before sunrise on the following morning. The trail was rough and we had to watch our step to avoid turning an ankle. The mountain trail was almost void of trees or vegetation, and so as the sun rose so did the temperature. The higher we climbed, the thinner the air became. Several boys passed out and we had to stop to revive them. Their packs were lightened by distributing their load among the others, and we climbed on.

Just before noon, we crossed over the craggy summit, panting, sweating, and worn out. However, renewed energy surged into us as we viewed a beautiful panorama of majestic wonder. More than 12,000 feet above sea level, high in the Sierras, was a mountain meadow unlike anything I had ever seen—even in a picture. Wild flowers and long green grasses stretched as far as the eye could see. Mountain peaks, crested with snow, seemed so close that we could touch them. The air never smelled more invigorating.

Something happened in my heart that day. I learned a valuable truth about the journey of life, the need for struggle, and the rewards of following the road less traveled. Taking that difficult, steep trail did not rob us of our goal, it enhanced and magnified it, making the rewards even sweeter.

As we struggle under the weight of our circumstances when the vision of our hopes and dreams grows dim, we must not forget the rewards of walking the road less traveled.

In life, each of us walks our own road. By our choices we turn at some crossroads, while the uncertainties and uncontrolled elements of life forcibly turn *us* at others. At times the way is easy and the burdens light, while at other times the way is rough and stony and our backs ache under the strain of a heavy load. It is during difficult circumstances that we wonder how we'll fare, or whether our dreams will ever be realized.

Dreams, however, are never destroyed by circumstances. Hopes and dreams are born in our hearts and minds and can only be destroyed there. While the difficulty of the way can make the light of hope flicker and dim, only we can ultimately cause it to fade away. Viktor E. Frankl, after suffering enormous atrocities in Jewish concentration camps under Nazi control in World War II, made this powerful observation, "Everything can be taken away from a man but one thing: the last of all human freedoms—to choose one's attitude in any given set of circumstances, *to choose one's own way*." (Viktor E. Frankl, *Man's Search For Meaning*, 1984, Simon & Schuster, p. 86, emphasis added.) Adversity does not need to lead us from our righteous ambitions, but closer to them. We have only to work, struggle, believe, and climb.

When we take the more difficult way, while the trail is stony and hard, the scenery before us may be magnificent and the rewards at the end of the way sweeter and more satisfying than ever before imagined. Without the miracle of time, and the difficulty of the way, we would be left to low valleys and common landscapes.

While walking the stony way, all our senses become more alive and increasingly sensitive. Even while taking the "road less traveled" we can find fulfillment and laughter along the way. Someone once said, "Surely God must have a sense of humor—he created us." With some help from hindsight, if we looked closely enough at some of the things we do, we'd find ourselves in stitches much of the time. Even during the hard times, life can be fun.

Recently, I went to an amusement park with my family and some friends. My brother, Paul, who was with us, helped lift me into the seat of each ride. We rode the roller coaster, the train, the water rides, and every other ride that looked entertaining. At the end of the day, we waited in line for the bumper cars.

Helping me into a bumper car, I had Paul leave me alone in my car while he got another one for himself. Using my arms, I lifted my leg and placed my foot directly over the accelerator pedal. Pushing down with my hand on my knee, I could control the forward movement of the bumper car. As the bell sounded and all the cars lurched forward, I pushed down on my knee and off I went. I steered with one hand and pushed down on my knee with the other.

At first, I tried to avoid getting hit by other cars. Soon, however, I was right in the heat of it, bumping head to head with everyone else. Every time I got hit, my foot would leave the accelerator and my leg would fly into the air. Regaining my balance, and trying to brace against other collisions, I would position my foot on the pedal and off I would go, seeking revenge. Suddenly, I'd get hit again from the side, and off my foot would fly. I would laugh and laugh as I tried to get positioned again.

Those who knew what I was doing, tried to keep me from my task, and so while trying desperately to reposition, they'd ram my car from the side, sending me falling over in my seat, laughing all the while. They laughed too. They should have—it was me who looked ridiculous! The final buzzer sounded the end of our ride, and it was time to go. Of all the rides that day, the bumper cars brought me the most pleasure and enjoyment.

Life is many times the same as that ride. As we climb into the car of life, we may, at first try to avoid every collision, every mishap. Soon, however, we realize that protection nullifies the purpose of the ride itself. Sure, the bumps are often hard, and when we are first hit, it makes our heads spin. However, recovering from the bumps, somehow we feel more alive. We laugh, we reposition ourselves, build our faith and strength, brace ourselves, and then get rammed again from the side. When it is all said and done, however, the ride of life should bring us great pleasure as we work through the processes of perfection and the knowledge of fulfilling a greater plan. Sure, the hard times came in my life. Absolutely, it got rough sometimes. But I had to remember that to avoid the bumps is to deny growth, happiness and life's purpose.

Life goes on. We laugh some, and we cry some. But we live with the knowledge that there was one far worthier and greater than ourselves who walked this way before. It is his plan we praise, his purposes we follow. A long time ago we all shouted for joy; today we should fall on our knees and thank our God who gave us life. The road is rough, but we can find comfort that someone has walked this way before.

There is no question that my life has been dramatically changed in many ways because of my accident years ago. However, one thing has remained consistent—the Lord has walked with me. With each challenge, each tear, each discovery, the Lord was there to share it with me. In ancient times, Jesus declared that he is "The Way." That doesn't mean he waits at the end of the road for us or will meet us somewhere along the trail. He is "The Way" and walks the stony path with us from the beginning until the end.

At times he has felt so close that I could sense his loving arms about me, while at other times I felt very much alone, feeling assurance only through his promise—but he has always been there. His influence and love have permeated every aspect of my life. No, I can't do everything I would like to do, or even feel a need to do. However, for what I must do, the Lord has granted me energy, resources and strength. What a contrast my life has been since those early days in the hospital. I may not be what I should be, or I may not be what I could be, but I thank God that I am not what I used to be.

Two years after leaving the hospital, I decided to go back for a visit and try my luck at the indoor one-eighth-mile track which I had struggled over in an effort to get a manual wheelchair. Exhausted, I had finished it in 28 minutes before. There was nobody there this time except me—no doctors, nurses, therapists, or even Dallas to encourage me. The tape was still on the floor, cracked and yellowing. Using the second hand on my watch to time myself, I took off. Exactly one minute and fifty-eight seconds later, I crossed that line again! Tears rolled down my cheeks as I reflected back over the months and years of effort, prayers, faith, and struggle which had brought me to this simple point in time and experience. I could not have felt happier. Some people would not call that a miracle, but I do.

In my travels I have passed many fellow sufferers. Some have greater physical handicaps than myself, others have lost their spouses to death, while others have lost them to sin. Some have suffered financial disaster, others have paid the price of uncontrolled wealth.

Each of us walks a path—sometimes easy and light, sometimes burdensome and heavy. If your path, right now, is easy and light, reach out to those who suffer. If your burdens are heavy and your path is stony, then reach out to God and find strength and peace in him. Once you have peace, share it with another who struggles, and you will witness your burdens becoming lighter.

The way is often stony and hard for a far greater purpose than we know. Without the difficulty of the way and the briars and the thorns of life's daily struggles, there would be no room for miracles, change, and growth in our mortal existence. While our faces show the pain of our circumstances, whether they be physical, mental, emotional, or spiritual; the power and mercy of one who loves us stands ready to reveal his mighty arm in our behalf that "the works of God might be made manifest" in our individual lives. This poem says it well:

"The road is too rough, dear Lord,"
I cried, "There are stones that hurt me so."
"My child," He said, "I understand,
I walked it long ago."

"But there's a cool green path ahead,
Let me walk there for a time."
"No child," He gently answered me,
"The green road does not climb."

"My burden," I cried, "is far too great.
How can I bear this load?"
"Dear One," said He, "I remember its
weight—I carried my cross, you know."

"But," I said, "I wish there were friends with me,
that would make their way my own."
"Oh yes," He said,
"Gethsemane was hard to bear alone."

And so I climbed the stony path,
Content at least to know
That where the Master had not gone,
I would not have to go.

And strangely then I found new friends,
My burdens grew less sore,
As I remembered long ago
He walked that way before.

(Author Unknown)

It's not the critic who counts, not the man who points out how the strong man stumbled or where the doer of deeds could have done better.

The credit belongs to the man who is actually in the arena, whose face is marred by dust and sweat and blood, who strives valiantly, who errs and comes short again and again, because there is no effort without err and shortcoming.

Who does actually strive to do the deed, who knows the great enthusiasms, the great devotions, spends themselves in a worthy cause; who, at the best knows in the end the triumph of high achievement and who at the worst, if he fails, at least fails while daring greatly, so that his place shall never be with those cold and timid souls who know neither victory nor defeat.

—Teddy Roosevelt —

Chapter Ten
Blood, Sweat, and Tears

"In the sweat of thy face shalt thou eat bread . . ." the Lord told Adam as he ushered him from the Garden of Eden. The significance of that declaration didn't have its full impact on me until after I had to return to work some six months after my accident. In one regard, I was extremely fortunate. My silent business partner and close friend held on to the construction and marketing company until I could run it again myself.

I had great desires and dreams built around the success of my new venture, but I knew I was going to need help. I called on Dallas's brother, Scott, and made him a business proposition. Before long, he packed his bags and moved from Utah to California to take an active role in the development of our dream.

Building and marketing tennis courts is extremely detailed and intensive work. During the five months prior to the accident, I had learned quite a lot about the successful operation of such a business. Now, it was my turn to teach it to someone else. Scott came daily to the hospital, and would sit beside my bed or my wheelchair, we would begin to go through the list of do's and don'ts, should's and should not's. We walked through the construction of a court step by step, detail by detail. Every conceivable problem was considered.

We continued to meet day after day. Scott would go to work, and then return the next day, with pages of questions and notes. The business began to grow.

Scott did a tremendous job of pulling the new business out of the stall the accident had created. Eventually, however, I needed to return to work. As soon as I was strong enough to endure sitting and working, I went back. My hours at first were scattered and inconsistent. I struggled with my ambitions and desires. Each day, Dallas would help me into my car, drive me to work an hour away, help me with the paperwork and other things I needed to do, then drive to her own job. She would come back to help me home again that evening. Work was just that it was work.

Scott would sell and supervise construction of the courts, and I would plan and execute home shows and marketing ideas. I also controlled the company books which was a new and uncomfortable responsibility for me. Although I came each day and did my work, my heart just wasn't in it. The ambitions I had before didn't burn as brightly. I needed a spark to set me on fire again. But I didn't expect the spark to be so disconcerting.

As I worked with the details of the business and with customers, I acquired a lot of good friends. Many of them held me in high regard for the effort I was expending. Many of them understood my limitations, but like real friends, they also saw my capabilities. However, not everybody was quite so sensitive or understanding.

Our company had been building a court for a family in Gilroy, some thirty miles from San Jose. It was a beautiful court, and a lot of time and effort was put into its construction. We were proud of the job we had done. However, we had one small problem. Our manufacturer failed to ship us the sports equipment required to play the games—a problem for the family, because they were planning a big birthday party on the court for their daughter.

Trying to be sensitive to that need, and having no other workers available, I got up early that Friday morning, threw my personal sports gear into an equipment bag, and headed for Gilroy. Perhaps my expectations were too high. I imagined that my customer would be pleased about the sacrifice I had made and would appreciate my concern for his needs. Those thoughts were shattered the instant my conversation with the father began.

"Where is my sports equipment?" the big man barked.

"Sir, I apologize that we don't have your personal equipment here today, it's been delayed in shipment. However,—" He cut me off,

"Well, that's just great! How am I supposed to play anything on the court with no equipment. You guys promised me I'd have it," he stewed angrily.

"Yes sir," I responded, "we did promise you equipment for your daughter's birthday party. Because of that, I have brought you my personal equipment to use until yours arrives." I smiled, hoping he would be pleased.

The father hesitated, not sure he wanted to stop being angry yet. He eyed me sitting far below him in the wheelchair, and then coldly replied, "Great, now that I have the sports equipment, who's going to demonstrate how to play the games to me—you?" Snatching the equipment bag from my lap, he swore bitterly, turned, and walked away.

My face flushed with anger. I felt hurt and disappointed. I hung my head and headed for my van. Traveling home, my mind played the words over and over again. The more I reflected on the incident, the hotter with anger I became. By the time I reached home, I was a time bomb just looking for a place to explode. "How could he say such things?" I questioned. "Doesn't he have any feelings or sensitivities to others?"

I concluded, however, that it was impossible for me to control other people and their actions. On the other hand, I *could* control me. This was *my* "road less traveled." Even if I felt he had acted inappropriately, I didn't need to act that way myself. Rather than carry a burden too great for me to bear, I decided to put my anger to a more useful purpose. Steam is capable of doing a lot more than just making noise in a tea kettle. It can move tons of steel!

I decided to make my steam move steel rather than just make noise. Instead of returning home, I drove to the office. As a result of my months of working with a struggling ambition, a pile of work had stacked up on my desk. Phone messages needed to be attended to, bills needed paying, and new marketing strategies planned. Allowing my anger to spark a rekindled ambition, I began my work with enthusiasm.

I worked all day and all night. Returning home Saturday morning, I had breakfast, changed my clothes, and returned to work again. That evening I spiritually knelt before the Lord and thanked him for that insensitive father who made an attack on my ego the day before. From that day on, I found new energy and strength to do the things I needed to do. My work became my joy, rather than my burden.

Fortunately, this irate father was the exception and not the rule. Most people I have met and worked with have been generous, compassionate and understanding. I have become accustomed to looks of pity as I push through a mall, and little children pointing a finger and innocently exclaiming, "Mom, look! There's a man in a wheelchair—why?" Yet even though people are intrigued by the tragedies of others, their hearts are usually warm and compassionate.

Whenever Dallas and I go out on the town together, which is often, we are overwhelmed by people's willingness to help. Our favorite movie theatre has a number of steep steps that must be climbed if you want good seats. I only have to sit at the bottom of those steps for a moment, before a couple of kind gentlemen—total strangers—will offer their assistance. Following the movie, instead of quickly leaving, they often search me out to help me down the stairs again.

Do you want to know the most valuable lesson I have learned through that experience? Even though a large variety of people have offered to help me, the first ones that always seem to step forward are the most unlikely. They are the big, tough, tattoo-laden bikers or "hippies" with the smell of cigarettes and alcohol on their breath. Often they're dirty and foul-mouthed. But, their hearts are bigger than they are. The depth of their compassion has been inconceivable to me. Society has rejected them. In the past I would have rejected them, too. But the road I have been traveling has given me a new perspective and has "made all the difference."

With the help of others, I am able to more fully realize and accomplish my dreams and deal with the necessities of life. People of all shapes and sizes offer their personal services to me ranging from helping me with a door, to cleaning my yard, to helping me move. The aged to the very young have all compassionately offered their hands in service. Each contributes to the miracles of another's life.

Discovering new abilities requires risk-taking and effort. Those who were willing to risk with me—customers, business associates, friends—found that not only was my heart willing, but my weak hands were often capable as well. I continued to operate the construction company for two years following my accident. We enjoyed tremendous success along with some humbling defeats throughout those two years. But we could see that the effects of my accident had taken their toll over time and the company had been too young to support two partners financially. Also, as we experienced dramatic increases in sales, my physical inability to contribute directly to the construction work led to mounting backlogs. Finally, we sold our business, Scott returned to school, and I went to find a new place in the work force.

This was a frightening experience for me. This was my first job-hunt since my accident. Before life in the wheelchair, finding good employment was easy and took only a small amount of effort. Now, it would require great effort, a lot of thought, good planning, and time. A doctor's words echoed in my ears, "Don't ever expect to work again, Art, because 93% of those in your condition never do."

The hardest thing was to decide for myself what I was able to do. What *could* I do that someone would be willing to pay money to have me perform? What talents and skills did I have to offer that made me a better choice than the next guy? Who would trust my abilities long enough to give me a fair shake at a job? However, I knew that somehow, somewhere, I would find my place.

I spent many hours scouring newspapers, calling employers, setting interviews and meeting with representatives of different companies. The story seemed like a never-ending circle. On the phone they would sound enthusiastic and promising regarding my qualifications, anxious for me to be a part of their team and sometimes almost even hiring me before we had a chance to interview. But then into their office I would roll, and their enthusiasm turned to disappointment and concern.

During the course of the interview, I would exert every effort to sell myself. I attacked their concerns up front, inviting questions and objections. To alleviate their business risk, I would offer to work for free for two weeks, even a month, to prove my capabilities. I told them if I could not perform as well, if not better, than their number one producer within one month, I would gladly leave their employ on my own accord. They seemed pleased with my willingness to sacrifice, but their level of trust and belief were aptly displayed through their lack of return phone calls or interviews. I kept looking.

After much effort, trying to find a place in the world of sales, I met with an experienced agency that assists physically limited people in getting jobs. Though they were very competent at what they do, they discouraged me from any further search in the sales field. They insisted that I was expecting too much—who would hire a quadriplegic to sell their products when they had plenty of able-bodied applicants to choose from? They asked me to lower my sights. I needed to work, so I applied for the position of a telephone operator for an IBM message center.

After several interviews with key people, and my list of usual promises and commitments, they said they would accept me if I had adequate typing competency. The job required a typing speed of no less than 40 words-per-minute. On the morning of the test, I was piled into a room with several others who would be testing as well. With typing splints firmly on my two index fingers, I began typing. Five minutes later the buzzer sounded the end of our test. I went home and waited for the return call. The call came and I was offered a three month temporary position with IBM. With superior performance, that period could be extended to six months. I needed that six month security; I had to give my best.

My new job consisted of taking internal messages for any of 9,000 employees at that plant site. I worked at a terminal along with about 15 other people. Our performance was measured by how many messages we were able to take each day. The phones would ring continually. As soon as you were done receiving a message for one person, the phone was ringing with the next. I took over 300 messages every day that I worked there, sometimes even exceeding 400, which broke previous records. I was given my three month extension.

Even though the Lord had blessed me with work temporarily, I needed challenging, permanent work with a future. Deep inside, the hope and dream of returning successfully to the world of sales had not diminished. I spent many hours praying for help in finding this kind of work. I needed a workplace that wasn't too far from home. I needed a healthy income to meet my financial obligations and medical needs. I needed good benefits including medical coverage. I needed a suitable work environment to meet the requirement of life in a wheelchair. My needs were great, but I knew the power of the Lord was greater.

Departing from the advice of the job counselors, I began my search again among computer sales companies. Instantly, I was met with rejection wherever I turned. Some simply never called back. Others told me very directly that, because I was in a wheelchair, I would not even be considered, regardless of any past achievements or sales records. It was often frustrating, yet I knew that with each rejection and denial would come benefits of equal or greater value. The rejections became the bread of hope I lived on. I could not be denied forever. The Lord and I would ultimately prevail.

Following dozens of interviews with technical companies,

the phone call finally came. "Art, we'd be excited to have you on our team. Bell Atlantic CompuShop has found a place for you. Can you start on Monday?" Tears flowed down my cheeks as I replied in the affirmative. My dream came true; a miracle had transpired. I thanked God for his divine intervention. I had a future I could build on.

The road, while still leading me to my hopes and dreams, did not promise an easy way. Each day required me to overcome the obstacles and barriers that stood in the way of my success and progress with Bell Atlantic CompuShop. Seeking strength from that same source which brought the miracle of good work into my life, together we defeated prejudice, tall counters, long hours, business travel to other states, and quotas.

I had discovered, as Dallas and I would go shopping together, that some people, uncomfortable with the fact that I was in a wheelchair, were more anxious to talk to Dallas than to me and would direct their conversations to her. "What is the warranty on your product?" I would ask. Looking into Dallas's eyes, they would respond to my inquiry

One salesman in his obvious discomfort, while Dallas and I sat together, asked, "What color do you think your husband would like that in?"

Dallas smilingly responded, "I don't know, why don't you ask him?" The salesman blushed.

This natural discomfort, which I experienced often with customers, could only be overcome through consistent application of human relation skills, patience, and a special attention to their individual needs. Every month that I was with the company I either met or exceeded my pre-set sales quota. I received national sales awards on three different occasions for my sales skills and achievements. When the company found it necessary to reduce its sales force by nearly 60%, I was one of two salesmen retained in our region. The Lord was revealing his mighty arm in my life. The seemingly impossible became reality.

The road to my sales success was unpaved, stony, and hard, but that road led me to my dreams. My dreams were not destroyed by my circumstances; they were made possible because of them. In all of my previous years of sales experience, never had any reward tasted so sweet or been as fulfilling as now.

As I struggled each day down this road not of my choosing, many of the activities and blessings I had been told were forever beyond my reach came back into my life. I was working again and building a promising financial future. I was sealed to the woman of my dreams for time and eternity. I had a new van adapted to my needs which I could drive by myself. I could go where I wanted to go and do what I wanted to do, independent of others. Leaving the experience of three and a half years of computer sales behind me, Dallas and I moved to Utah to fulfill another dream.

Despite my success in the computer sales world, I had long retained the desire to be in business for myself again—to be financially independent. During my years in computer sales, I searched for opportunities, and worked to prepare myself financially, mentally, and technically. While a teenager, I was profoundly impacted by positive books and audio cassette programs. They made such a difference in my attitude, aptitude, and desires! They became my passion for many years as I was working to become the man I knew I should and could be.

In time, the elements necessary to fulfill my dreams came together, and my years of searching and waiting were over. I opened a retail bookstore in the Salt Lake City area. Surrounded by the object of my passion and love—books and tapes—I was better prepared to set myself on the path of the entrepreneur again. By doing so, I was also able to fulfill

141

another dream, by having a business in which Dallas and I could work, share, and build together. And we *are* building, as we have since opened two additional bookstores and started a small international mail-order company which manufactures a product for wheelchair users. Lemonade really does come from lemons—that's one of the miracles of life.

In moving to Utah, Dallas and I were able for the first time to purchase our own home, having it custom-built to meet the specific needs of life in a wheelchair: hardwood floors in the heavy traffic areas to make rolling around the house easier, oversized bathrooms, an elevator to raise me from one level to the next, and ramps built-in to accommodate my entry into the home.

Adversity is not the enemy. Victory can still be won, our dreams fulfilled, if we are willing to work, struggle, believe, and wait. As we struggle under the weight of our burdens through the course of time, seeking the miracles which come, we begin to feel as Winston Churchill did when he declared, "I have nothing to offer but blood, toil, tears and sweat." Given those individual ingredients plus the necessary time, we are assured a victor's crown.

While facing a seemingly invincible Nazi enemy, Churchill went on to say, "We have before us an ordeal of the most grevious kind. We have before us many, many months of struggle and of suffering. You ask what is our policy? I will say: It is to wage war, by sea, land, and air, with all our might and with all our strength that God can give us . . . That is our policy. You ask, what is our aim? I can answer in one word: Victory—victory at all costs, victory in spite of terror; victory, however long and hard the road may be." (*Churchill: The Life Triumphant*, American Heritage, 1965, p. 90.)

The road, while it has been long and hard, has been marked

by milestones, plateaus, and individual triumphs which were required before victory, in any measure, could be achieved.

These small triumphs, have become the miracles along the way which have made the view more glorious and the fruit more sweet.

Then said David to the Philistine, Thou comest at me with a sword, and with a spear, and with a shield: but I come to thee in the name of the Lord of hosts, the God of the armies of Israel, whom thou hast defied.

This day will the Lord deliver thee into mine hand; and I will smite thee, . . . that all the earth may know that there is a God in Israel.

And all this assembly shall know that the Lord saveth not with sword and spear: for the battle is the Lord's, and he will give you into our hands.

(1 Samuel 17:45-47.)

Chapter Eleven
Conquering My Goliaths

"Yes, I'd be honored," was my answer in response to a cautiously asked question posed by a member of the bishopric. They wanted me to become an early-morning seminary teacher for the stake. Dallas stared at me with the thought clearly written in her eyes, "But, how?" The man smiled calmly, thanked us, shook our hands, and said my materials would be brought over during the week. Shutting the door behind him, he was on his way.

Now, Dallas asked the question which had been pounding itself over and over again in her mind, "How, Art, how are you going to do it?"

My answer was less than comforting. I responded, "I don't know."

Just months before my accident, I had been asked to be an early-morning seminary teacher in our ward in Hollister, California. Even though being a seminary teacher had long been a dream and ambition of mine, I reluctantly had to decline. All my circumstances made it impossible for me to accept at the time. I was to be married in only two months, and then I'd be moving to another stake. My newly formed tennis court construction company was requiring twelve to sixteen hours a day of my time, six days a week. As much as I wanted to accept, prudence demanded that I say, "No." Only weeks

145

later I was involved in the accident which left me paralyzed. But the surrendering of that dream left a hole in my heart I was afraid would never be filled again. I wanted to be a seminary teacher, but I thought they'd never ask me now.

The counselor in the bishopric of our San Jose, California, ward was led more by the spirit than most men I had encountered. When the need for a new seminary teacher was announced, the spirit whispered his course of action. Despite his eagerness to make the call, he was met with resistance from those who were concerned with the obvious questions. How will Art do it? Is he independent enough? Can he get to the church that early every morning? Can he keep up with the preparation and presentation of materials five days a week for months? How will he control a class of twenty students? To a man like that counselor there was only one answer, when the spirit whispers—respond! Little did anyone realize the miracles which would transpire in the life of a struggling quadriplegic when a faithful brother asked a simple and open question directed by the Lord himself, "Art, will you accept the invitation to be an early-morning seminary teacher?"

Now, Dallas and I were left to our own thoughts and concerns. We had a problem to resolve, a problem which had evaded a solution now for more than four years. Having limited use of arms and hands, dressing myself entirely had always been a challenge that defied solution. From the first days and weeks in the hospital the words of the doctors and therapists echoed clearly in my ears, "You'll always need someone to help you. Wherever you go, whatever you do, you'll never be fully independent again. Get used to it."

For four years I battled that haunting echo in my mind as I learned to drive again, began to earn an income, to get myself from place to place, to prepare my own meals and many other

146

seemingly small details which were in reality to me significant faith-promoting miracles. Yet, every morning on every day of the year I had to have help to dress for the day's activities. I had been told there was no other way.

Now I sat before that obstacle which stood as a giant Goliath before the small David and wondered perhaps what small, smooth stones the Lord had prepared for my sling. On this one mountain of challenge hung the hopes and dreams of a young man's past.

"Yes," had been my response to the bishopric's question, and so now there was only one choice available: solve the problem. With anxious hearts and sometimes doubting minds, Dallas and I approached the Lord. There was no audible answer, no voice from heaven or angels ministering—only the comforting influence of the spirit that our course was right.

My father and brother helped me construct a padded platform which would serve as the firm surface I needed. Taking from my wardrobe those clothes which seemed to be the loosest and easiest to put on, I began to work at the challenging job of dressing myself, from pants and shirt to socks and shoes.

Seminary started at 6:15 every weekday morning. To be prepared and have the classroom set up for the lesson, I needed to leave my home before 5:30 a.m. I arose at 2:30 a.m. that first morning to attempt the task. In my younger years, I had wrestled with a lot of things: my brother, the influence of the evil one, and with difficult decisions, but I had never once experienced wrestling with myself—especially not for two and a half hours! Using every available resource: teeth, arms, shoulders, and hands with fingers that refused to work, I struggled to get dressed. Throughout the ordeal, I found myself softly calling out, "Lord, please help me. I need thee." Even with every physical resource expended to its fullest, without the unseen resources of faith, desire, and priesthood power, I would still be wrestling on that platform today. But by 5:30 that morning, physically exhausted and spiritually spent, I sat dressed and ready for seminary, with one more "Goliath" conquered—a milestone achieved, a plateau reached.

During the ensuing weeks and months, the process which once required every ounce of courage and strength I possessed, along with the penalty of two and a half hours of time, now required less than twenty minutes. For the next year and a half I taught early-morning seminary. It was a dream that was now coming true.

Tremendous power and satisfaction came from teaching and sharing with those remarkable young minds every morning of the week. I came to love those young people. The daily hours of prayer and study required to teach such a course of study brought me closer to my Savior in more meaningful ways than could have come to me by any other road. The blessing of that miracle has poured its influence upon every other avenue of my life. While it might seem a small thing, it has become one of the pinnacles of my experience.

Working within the limits of our individual human capacity, our abilities are stretched through the faithful exercising of hope, priesthood power, prayer, and righteous desires to the accomplishing of all things which are right for us in our lives. If our desires are appropriate and the Lord's will is manifest, then the reality of our limitations pale next to the power of the Lord's arm in achieving and overcoming all things. When I speak of these things, I am not limiting the influence of miracles to only spiritual ends, but to all areas of our multi-faceted lives. When the Lord declared that to him, "all things are spiritual," I smile at the realization that "all" includes even such pursuits as "Quad Rugby."

Played on a basketball court with a volleyball, four wheelchairs on either side face each other. (Of course, there are people in the wheelchairs!) The game itself is restricted to quadriplegics, thus giving it the title "Quad Rugby." Many quadriplegics have injuries so extensive that they are unable to play the game, so I felt fortunate to be participating.

The object of the game is to get the ball across a goal line (which is fifteen feet wide at the other end of the court) while you maintain control of it. To get the ball there, you can roll it, throw it, bounce it, or pass it to another team member. However, a player must have control of the ball when he or she crosses the goal line for it to be considered a scoring drive. Those who have not watched the game have missed a unique visage of athletics. With total disregard to what they can or cannot do, athletes race from one end of the court to the other, bumping, colliding, grabbing, swinging, and picking—as they'd say it in basketball. There is no such word as "quit" when eight quadriplegics of varying classifications are let loose on one court.

During an exhibition match for fun with another team, every player was caught up in the vigor and competitive spirit of the game. On defense, it was my job to watch the left side of the goal line—to keep the ball and players out. On offense, the other team's strategy was to send all four players at the goal line as fast as they could. Realizing that we couldn't block the entire line altogether, at the last minute the point man would pass the ball to the player with the best opportunity and opening. Upon catching and keeping the ball, the player's speed and momentum alone would carry him across the goal line.

My pulse quickened as, in the final moment, the ball came to my side. However, the ball was just outside the reach of my opponent. As he stretched his arms and torso to pull the ball into his lap, his chair went up onto just two wheels, leaving him off-center and unbalanced. However, if he caught and maintained control of the ball, his speed and momentum would carry him victoriously across the goal line. There seemed to be only one solution—I pushed him over.

Now, don't worry too much about the other guy. He wasn't hurt much. He cut his leg just a bit, but he couldn't feel it anyway! I guess it was fair for them to throw me into the penalty box for a couple of minutes. Later, I had a good laugh with the athlete I had pushed. It made us both feel good to be involved in a game where we weren't protected from the rough realities of sports. We felt alive and invigorated while pushing, maneuvering, and playing; it felt great just to play a competitive game again. Later, our little team traveled to Dallas, Texas, to compete nationally.

Playing Quad Rugby involved risk—but for me even going to a certain friend's home for an evening of games, food, and fun involves risk! The entry into their apartment has a dozen steps going down. One night, as usual in this scenario, I had to have two friends, grabbing the front and back of the wheelchair, slowly carry my chair and myself down the steps. My brother, who had also been invited, was on the back of the chair, and a friend held the front. Before the effort began, I gave precise instructions of each carrier's responsibility, coupled with a little humor. I explained, "The job of the man carrying the back is to bear most of the weight, set the pace as we go, and make a covenant to *never* let go! The man up front has one principle responsibility—in the event that the man in back is unfaithful and drops the chair with me in it, the front man is to sacrifice his body in an effort to save me! Are we understood?" Both responded reassuringly.

No sooner had we begun the descent, when my brother

slipped on a step and began to fall forward. The friend, seeing me and my wheelchair falling toward him, instinctively jumped clear of our path! Falling, rolling, bumping, banging, I made my way ungracefully to the bottom, my brother still clinging desperately to an empty chair as he fell behind me. With only minor bumps and bruises, we all still laugh about it to this day. To risk is to live, laugh, and love.

I felt alive again as I competed in sports once more. My doctors and therapists had always rejected the idea of any athletics or competition for me with my disability. To feel my muscles work and fight again, even in their limited way, was more satisfying than I can express.

Quad Rugby became a door swinging wider for me as I later enjoyed snowskiing on a sled-like ski with short poles in my hands (we call it "sit-skiing"), swimming, and tennis. My family says I swim . . . just like a *rock*! That's okay, at least I have learned to hold my breath really well. When the family goes to the lake, I drive the boat with competitive skiers in tow.

Each of these activities once represented enormous "Goliath's" of impossibility in my limited life, but now stand as witness to a miracle brought about by time, effort, and priesthood power. Why a miracle? Because if left to my own power and capabilities, the activities I now enjoy would have remained the overpowering giant of hopes lost.

Perhaps the significance of these events would be clearer if you understood more intimately the barriers of cause and effect in the life of a quadriplegic. They are simple things, but often represent a gap which forever separates the world of possibility from the dreams of probability.

One of a myriad of problems is that my body doesn't sweat anymore. I know that to a young person at a youth dance that probably sounds like a miracle in itself. And, believe me, it can have its advantages. I am sure I have saved a bundle of money on deodorant; however, it also has its problems.

Not being able to sweat, which is the body's natural mechanism for cooling off, means that the body temperature quickly rises with the outside temperature. While engaged in active sports or when exposed too long to high outside temperatures, the body gets hotter and hotter, bringing the possibility of heat stroke and even death. The signs of danger come when the breathing gets labored and heavy, the eyes get glossy, the body becomes extremely weak, and the head is light.

One hot, sunny afternoon in San Jose, California, outside temperatures rose to a sweltering 107 degrees, while inside our poorly insulated home it was even hotter. For three hours I wore a path in the carpet between the cool running water of the bathroom sink and the fan whirring at high speed. I would completely soak my head under the cold water and then contentedly sit directly in front of the fan. Still, after three hours of this, my body temperature continued to rise and I began to suffer the danger signs.

Time was not on my side as the minutes ticked away my options. I quickly pushed myself outside, got into my van, and headed for one place I knew I could find ultimate relief—the grocery store. Wheeling weakly through the automatic doors, I felt the rush of environmentally controlled cool air whisper across my face and neck. But, I knew right where I needed to head. I went in the direction of the frozen food section. Pulling the glass doors open, I laid my head right down on the frozen corn. Ahhhhh! I could have lived there all day. However, in moments, shoppers began to gather and look oddly at my posture. Fearing I would discourage frozen corn sales, I left my bastion of comfort and made my way to another source of relief, the meat department.

Finding the butcher, I announced, "I'm in serious trouble, and need to cool down fast, sir. May I please sit in your meat freezer?" With a puzzled look, he gestured for me to follow as we entered through a doorway of mist and escaping cold air. Now, sitting alongside frozen sides of beef and with my breath showing in the crisp air, the effects of the heat began to diminish.

However, only minutes later, the butcher returned and apologetically responded, "I'm sorry, sir, but I am afraid that if I leave you in here much longer you'll end up looking like one of the sides of beef. That would not reflect well on my job. But, if you'll follow me I have a better solution."

Moments later I sat in the cool air of the dairy locker behind rows of milk, cottage cheese, and yogurt. The danger of my situation passed and my mind became clear again. I figured that as long as I was here, I might as well have some fun. As shoppers reached their hands toward the yogurt, from behind the strawberry flavor they heard a voice, distinct and commanding, "Don't buy the strawberry. Get me, the vanilla!" Shoppers looked hesitantly to the right and left, and then stared into the rows of yogurt trying to find the source of the voice they were sure they heard. Mystery unsolved, they gently loaded their carts with vanilla yogurt. While I sold a ton of yogurt that hot afternoon, the grocery store manager didn't pay me any commissions, but he did invite me back again!

Despite the challenges and threats of disabling limitations, through the balancing of caution and risk, faith and reality, effort and time, the world of sports and competition opened the windows of opportunity again to my view. I began training for wheelchair racing and started to compete in organized races and marathons. Nothing I have ever done causes me to sense the powerful arm of the

Almighty working more in my life than when he lifts me from one plateau of physical accomplishment to another. It is hard to convey the witness of the spirit which arises from such seemingly ordinary activities.

Reflections by Dallas

I stood at the finish line, nervously pacing. I was trying to control my feelings of worry and concern, but scenes of a race years past now kept my mind anxiously whirling. At Art's first race, two years ago, he had been the last to finish. Runners and wheelchair racers had all completed the five mile course and were leaving for home when Art had come into sight. Race organizers had been busy taking down the sign marked, "finish." So, how would it be this time? Crowds of people stood around me now, also waiting. This was to be Art's first ten-kilometer (6.2 mile) race, and I wondered who would still be here when he crossed the finish line. Down the road, I could see the first runners battling for the finish. I saw their strong, lean legs pumping, their faces the epitome of concentration. The crowds cheered them on as they crossed. I felt my emotions rise to see the wonder of the human body—to see it extend and push beyond natural capacity. Art's new light-weight racing chair had arrived only two days before, and he hadn't even had a chance to train or get familiar with it. As he sat in it for the first time, it felt awkward to both of us. Would he be able to push and maneuver his way adequately? Now, more and more runners were coming in, faces red and exhausted. Then, I saw something that made my heart jump. Down the road was a wheelchair, coming in fast. It wasn't Art's, but I was surprised to see a wheelchair racer so soon.

I knew Art had been blessed with strength and health unusual for people of his level of disability. Still, I didn't know all Art *could* do until only forty-eight minutes into this race.

With eyes strained and a hopeful heart, I recognized Art's form moving toward me up the street. Rather than inching his way painfully forward as he had done in the first race, he was steadily pulling away from the runners as the finish line drew nearer and the cheers from the waiting crowd were ringing in my ears. A wave of emotion washed over me as I sank to my knees, my eyes flooded with tears. How could this be? Two years before, a five-mile race had taken him two-and-a-half hours to complete; now it took him less than an hour for more than six miles!

The other wheelchair entrants were all paraplegics, able to grasp and grip the rings as they pushed with the back, shoulder, stomach, and tricep muscles working in perfect unison and harmony, and yet Art, using only the back of his hand and wrist to propel himself, came in only minutes behind. With a summer full of other ten-kilometer races, the strength that had been given Art would further reveal The Lord's hand in our lives. Art would come in third place in the Deseret News 10K, ahead of several other paraplegics. These triumphs became a personal testimony to us as we saw miracles build upon each other day after day. Knowing we should thank God for all things gave us the perspective needed to see these small wonders in our lives and enabled us to praise and thank our Father for his merciful hand.

Muscles tensed in the cold, dark air of the morning. We could see our breath and it seemed to fill the crisp air as runners shook and stretched their legs to loosen up. An intensity was mounting as minutes ticked away, but no one spoke. A soft glow was filling the horizon as the sun crept toward the new morning sky. In front of the throng of runners were the eight wheelchair competitors, adjusting their helmets, securing the tape around wrists and hands, and making final changes to their tucked seating positions.

A gun sounded in the clear morning air and eight wheelchairs and fifteen hundred runners lunged forward to begin the long and arduous race toward St. George, Utah, some 26.2 miles away. Holding pace with the other wheelchairs, I tried to establish a reasonable rhythm that I could maintain for the next several hours. The St. George marathon is considered a fast course for wheelchair participants with its rolling hills and eventual decline into the valley. However, while moments of rest were welcomed as the terrain temporarily turned its course downward, I knew that the steep climbs could make all the difference in finishing at all. In my mind I could clearly see the words of an article I had read time and time again over the years I had lived in a wheelchair. It spoke of a three hour barrier as though it were the Berlin wall. Like Roger Bannister of the track world, the article talked about those wheelchair athletes who, after years of training, had broken beyond the limits of expectation to set new records below the three hour mark. The blood flowed into my shoulders as I surged past the wheelchair racer beside me.

The chair I was now securely tucked into was so different from the one I use everyday. It weighed only nine pounds and was black and hot pink. I wore black and hot pink stretch pants, with a black helmet, hot pink tank top and black and hot pink sun glasses. Dallas figured that if I wasn't going to win, at least I ought to look good. The chair has three wheels and I race with my knees tucked into my chest. Since I have no grip in my hands, I use a backhand pushing technique to maintain speed and momentum.

The sun suddenly broke out over the mountain peaks and eight wheelchairs leaned into a sharp corner together, still traveling as a pack. As we neared the seven mile marker, I saw the hill I had been warned of looming defiantly before me and I took a deep breath as I speedily approached. As soon as the ascent began, the pack instantly pulled away from me. I was quadriplegic, they were paraplegic, and the hill would prominently display the difference. Without hand strength to grip the ring, and no right tricep to endure the climb, I slowed to a crawl. The hill was so steep that if I raised my head from my knees even an inch, my front wheel began to rise off the road. If someone had told me then that climb would continue for the next five miles, I probably would have quit right there. But with ignorance as my companion—and faith, desire and hope as my friends—I slowly inched my way up the hill. The three hour barrier was no longer my concern. That obstacle would have to await another day to be challenged. For now, I just wanted to finish the race, no matter how long it took.

My muscles strained and ached, and my shoulders began to feel numb. The tape from my wrists had worn down and my gloves began to slip from my hands. The sun beat down relentlessly and my body temperature began to rise. I looked up the road and watched as it continued its steep climb, curving out of sight. All the warning signs began to go off, and I knew I was facing an uncomfortable decision. Again, glancing up the road, careful to keep my chin to my knee, I thought to myself, "I will push just one hundred more times, and then I will quit. I mean, who would blame me? This is the farthest I have ever gone." Slowly, methodically, I began the long count, "One . . . two . . . three . . . ." I inched my way up the road. After reaching one hundred, I looked again at the continuing climb and thought, "I'll push just one hundred more times, and then I'll stop. The relief vehicles can take me to the finish line and I will still have won a great battle. Who would expect me to finish anyway? One . . . two . . . three . . . ." Runner after runner began to pass me, and I experienced what has become the central message of this story and every story of human suffering and sacrifice. The effect was so profound as to leave my cheeks wet with tears as I made my way slowly forward. As runners passed, I felt their hands slap my shoulders and the back of my helmet (some almost knocked me from my chair!) and from their lips came these words on the wind, "Come on, chair! Don't give up, chair. You can make it, chair. Come on, chair." As the runners made their way past me, their words echoed in my ears. They may never know the spiritual impact they had on one simple life. Their words of compassion and hope reflected the years of my personal struggle.

I realized then how every struggle, every tear, every outcry for help has been met with words of encouragement whispered by the spirit, "Come on, Art! Don't give up, Art. You can make it, Art. Come on, Art." That morning the words of each of those sincere and compassionate runners became the voice of God himself to me. My strength became renewed, and reaching into depths of ability and endurance I had not previously possessed, I moved the chair forward. Gloves slipping, blisters forming, and muscles ready to collapse, thousands of pushes later I learned one very valuable truth— with every up, there is a down, and I passed all of those dear runners at 38 miles per hour! With sirens ringing clearly in the morning air, a highway patrolman on a motorcycle raced in front of me to keep the road clear as I surged forward to try and catch the other chairs which were miles ahead.

I did finish that race, and as I crossed the line, hundreds of anxious observers cheered the efforts of a man with a face that showed signs of utter exhaustion. The clock read two hours and fifty-three minutes and fifty-four seconds. The three-hour wall had fallen.

That race has become symbolic of the miracle of my adversity. It is one of the fruits which hangs from a tree I must now declare as good. Using time and effort to my advantage, along with strength given by a loving Father, I have begun to train for a race which symbolizes an even higher plateau of opportunity and growth. It's appropriately called, "The Race of the Midnight Sun." Esteemed as the longest marathon in the world, the course stretches from Fairbanks, Alaska, to Anchorage, Alaska, and is held during the month of July each year. It is a nine day, 367 mile "Goliath" which less than forty wheelchair racers have finished in more than seven years.

The new wall? No quadriplegic of my classification has yet crossed the finish line. Why would I try it? Because it glorifies him who has brought me this far and stands as a witness that given time, effort and the power of a God who loves us, all things that lie within his perfect will for us, or that we righteously desire, are possible. They become the miracles along the way which give us perfect hope for a brighter day.

When I lay in that bed in the Las Vegas hospital with a broken neck, I wondered if all my hopes, dreams, and ambitions had been broken with it. My new future was carefully explained to me in painful detail. None of the plans included working, driving a vehicle, getting married and enjoying a fulfilling relationship, being independent, or participating in the sports I loved. It seemed that an enormous obstacle prevented the realization of hopes and dreams important to me. But only a detour was being laid out; a detour which, through effort, time, and priesthood power, would lead me to my desires. I never imagined, however, how much sweeter my real victories would be than those I originally dreamed of, or how much more beautiful the view.

All paths which have been or must be,
Must pass through Gethsemane.
All those who journey, soon or late,
Must pass somewhere through the garden's gate.
Must kneel alone in darkness there,
And deal with some fierce despair.
God pity those who cannot say,
"Not mine, but thine," who only pray
"Let this cup pass," and cannot see
The purpose of Gethsemane.

(Author Unknown)

Chapter Twelve
Bearing Good Fruit

While speaking at a youth conference in Louisiana, a young man asked me a very pointed, but honest question. "What is a miracle?" He asked innocently, with a deep desire to truly know. I told him that miracles are simply those things which, without the direct intervention of the power and priesthood of God, we could not perform by our own strength or resources. Whether that means restoring sight to a blind man, parting the waters of the Red Sea, taking the hate and venom from the heart of a mother whose husband was brutally murdered in cold blood, or enabling a weak and paralyzed quadriplegic to stretch beyond his limited abilities to the realization of his otherwise unattainable dreams, the formula is the same. While varying in power and display, all require the mercy and power of a loving Father and a compassionate Savior.

A retarded child learning to write is no less a significant miracle than stopping of the sun for a day since both accomplishments were beyond the natural reach of the individual involved and only possible through the Lord's intervention.

Was it a miracle when Moses parted the waters of the Red Sea and two million people crossed on dry ground? Surely it was. When Elijah called down fire from heaven to consume a worthy sacrifice, was it a miracle? Yes. When Jesus laid his hands upon the sick and they were healed; the deaf and they heard; the lame, and they walked, were those miracles? Absolutely!

But is it a miracle when a small caterpillar grows and evolves and becomes a beautiful butterfly? By the laws of nature that we are aware of, it is. And was it a miracle when a young boy walked from a grove of trees in 1820 and the results of his testimony alone have swelled to a church which now exceeds more than seven million members? I'd say, absolutely.

Then what is the difference between the two types of miracles? The only difference is time. In our modern age of technology, complete with jet propulsion, automobiles, space shuttles, computers, and fax machines, information and people race from one end of our world to the other at inconceivable speeds. In a day where tomorrow is interpreted as too late and "now" has become the operative word in business, the concept of time has taken on a distorted meaning.

We live in an "instant" world. A world where if you cannot have it now, do it now, or enjoy it now, it is esteemed as being of little value. In the Church, this translates into the understanding that a miracle must happen instantaneously to be regarded as a miracle.

While we eagerly plant our gardens and fruit trees with the full realization that they will eventually produce *in their season*, we expect the priesthood and our faith to always produce instantaneous results. That expectation comes from a myth, a lie, taught only by the voice of Satan.

The essentail ingredient of many miracles we call time, Satan has labeled a curse which he espouses as repulsive. The greatest blessings have come into my own life only after long effort, hard work, priesthood power and time. Elder Boyd K. Packer said, "Some people think a miracle is only a miracle if it happens instantaneously, but miracles can grow slowly, and patience and faith can compel things to happen that otherwise never would have come to pass."

As my mind reflects back to the life of Joseph Smith, I am reminded that at the age of fourteen he brought his questions to the Lord regarding which of all the churches were true. In glorious light, this young boy was told by the Savior himself that he must join none of the churches. However, if he would remain faithful, God would restore his true church and kingdom once again upon the earth through him. The light faded as he was once again left alone.

With a fourteen-year-old boy's limited perception of time, Joseph was left to wait. I suppose, to his young mind and heart, Christmas probably seemed an eternity away. How soon do you think he anticipated the return of his Lord in restoring the truth to the earth as he had promised? Tomorrow? Next week? Or perhaps even next month?

How long did young Joseph wait? It was three years before he was visited again by heavenly messengers of truth and light. Moroni visited him then, introducing the Book of Mormon—which was still upon the plates of gold. For four years, Moroni continued to visit Joseph before he was allowed to receive the plates. It was an additional three years, totaling ten in all, before the Lord's church and kingdom were ultimately established again here on the earth.

Certainly, nobody would argue that fulfillment of all the prophecies concerning the restoration would be a miracle of enormous proportions. Yet, it was prophesied more than two thousand years ago. Time plays an essential role in the working of miracles.

I believe that the one consistent ingredient in all the promises the Lord had made to Joseph Smith was that he would have to wait. Everything Joseph received, it seems, he waited for.

History records that, at times, Joseph became impatient in "waiting upon the Lord," but the Lord was building a prophet as much as he was building his kingdom. Even as Joseph suffered in the Liberty Jail for a season, he became weary of his anguish. In desperation he cried out, "Oh God, where art thou? And where is the pavilion that covereth thy hiding place?" His next big questions in this cry for help began time and again with the words, "How long . . . ?" (D&C 121: 1,2.)

There were many occasions when I, too, became "weary in my suffering." There were many times when I echoed the words of the prophet Joseph, particularly in my application of the words, "How long . . . ?"

But slowly, because of the things I experienced, I came to understand and realize the great benefits and miracles which come through the process of waiting. As I learned to "wait upon the Lord," he schooled me in those things which would produce true happiness and joy. He provided tools for me to work with and friends and family to help along the way. I could have chosen to be bitter, instead of choosing to learn; but the blessings that have already rolled down from my experiences have outweighed the pain and anguish, the discomfort and inconvenience. The miracle is in the journey perhaps even more than in the destination itself.

Faith and persistence are growing things. And in my growing, I continually focused upon the promises made to Joseph Smith in his darkest hour: "My son, peace be unto thy soul; thine adversity and thine afflictions shall be but a small moment; And then, if thou endure it well, God shall exalt thee on high; thou shall triumph over all thy foes." (D&C 121:7,8.)

President Spencer W. Kimball has said that there are

"infinitely more miracles today than in any age past and just as wondrous." Then where are they and why do you and I seem to miss them? Where are those instantaneous miracles of yesteryears? But, *were* they instantaneous?

As we walk along the dusty roads of ancient Jerusalem through the words and images of the scriptures, we read that as Jesus and his disciples passed by the temple walls, they came upon a man who had been blind from birth. For years he had come there, hoping that a deliverer, such as Elisha, would one day come. And so each day he waited.

As Jesus passed by, the disciples asked, "Master, who did sin, this man or his parents, that he was born blind?" With infinite knowledge he responded, "Neither hath this man sinned, nor his parents: *but that the works of God should be made manifest in him*." (John 9:2,3 emphasis added.) Using the moisture from his own spittle, he formed from the dust of the earth clay whereby he anointed the blind man's eyes. In a voice filled with compassion and foresight he commanded the man, "Go, wash in the pool of Siloam."

As quickly as any blind man can make his way through the obstacles and crowds of a bustling marketplace, he went in the immediate direction of the pool. Cupping his hands together he gathered the healing water to his face. As the water fell, his eyes were flooded with light. Eyes once shut with darkness now had a new view of the world. What a miracle! Who could not sense the significant blessing which had come into this simple man's life. Surely, he would never be the same again.

I don't know how old the blind man was, but was the miracle of his life just an "instant" thing? Was it the miracle of a day or an hour or even a moment? Or was it the concluding event of a miracle that took a lifetime? Through the vision of our own finite perspective, do we look upon the one act as though it stood alone, independent of a lifetime of hopes, prayers, growth, faith, and miracles?

How many of us have read the splendor of the Lord's miracles in the Old and New World, both in modern and ancient times and have ached to feel the power of his healing touch in our own lives? Even today there are those who are blind, or lame, or diseased and whose hearts and lips have extended toward the heavens in question and desire, seeking the power of the Savior's healing touch. And then there are those who have broken hearts and homes, discouragement and rejection, frustration and misery, and who struggle daily to find meaning and hope. Each seeks the healing touch. Each wonders how to obtain the power of the Master. Some still hope for the light, while others see only darkness.

Regardless of the circumstances or struggle, each battles against a common enemy—time. Minutes pass slowly and days seem to extend forever when we struggle under the burdens of suffering, adversity, or pain. Time becomes the adversary, reluctant to release us from its grasp. As the minutes blend into hours, the hours into days, and the days into years, the purpose and meaning of it all becomes vague and distorted.

Yet, the greatest miracle of all is that you and I can change and grow while we sojourn in this mortal probation. The miracle of change and growth has been reserved for mankind and his eternal offspring alone. No other of God's creatures, large or small, can make this glorious claim. Without time and experience, the process of change and growth would become frustrated and impossible. If every blessing bestowed, every healing delivered, and every righteous exercising of the Lord's priesthood produced "instantaneous" results, we would be robbed of the fundamental element of time which produces the opportunity for growth. We would then be denied the greatest miracle of all—the transformation of our hearts, minds, souls, and habits. How many years and months the blind man suffered we do not know. Which was the greater miracle, the opening of his darkened eyes, or the myriad of opportunities for change and growth which were given him only through the miracle of those years of waiting?

If our lives were left absent of struggle, suffering, adversity, pain, and anguish, would miracles exist at all? And if in the finality of life, we pass beyond, having never personally witnessed the majesty and power of the Lord's mighty arm as it is revealed in some of our darkest hours, then a tragedy truly has occurred.

Thomas Edison devoted ten years and all of his money to developing the nickel alkaline storage battery at a time when he was almost penniless. Through that period of time, his record and film production company was supporting the storage battery effort. Then one night the terrifying cry of "Fire!" echoed through the film plant. Spontaneous combustion had ignited some chemicals. Within moments all of the packing compounds, celluloid for records, film, and other flammable goods had gone up in flames. Fire companies from eight towns arrived, but the heat was so intense and the water pressure so low that the fire hoses had no effect. Edison was sixty-seven years old—no age to begin anew. His daughter was frantic, wondering if he was safe, if his spirit was broken, how he would handle a crises such as this at his age. She saw him running toward her. He spoke first. He said, "Where's your mother? Go get her. Tell her to get her friends. They'll never see another fire like this as long as they live!" At five-thirty the next morning, with the fire barely under control, he called his employees together and announced, "We're rebuilding." One man was told to lease all the machine shops in the area, another to obtain a wrecking crane from the Erie Railroad Company. Then, almost as an afterthought, Edison added, "Oh, by the way. Anybody know where we can get some money?"

Virtually everything we now recognize as a Thomas Edison contribution to our lives came *after* that disaster. (Jeffrey Holland, *However Long and Hard the Road*, Deseret Book, 1989, p.3.) Good fruit filled the sagging branches of Edison's tree. He very likely accomplished *because* of his tragedy, not in spite of it.

Someone once candidly asked me, "How can you talk positively about something that happened to you which is so bad?" My answer is simple. Can good come of evil? If this accident and the experiences I have had because of it can be regarded as "evil," then my answer is yes. Yet the Savior, during his mortal ministry in Old Jerusalem said: "Even so every good tree bringeth forth good fruit; but a corrupt tree bringeth forth evil fruit. A good tree cannot bring forth evil fruit, neither can a corrupt tree bring forth good fruit. *Wherefore by their fruits ye shall know them.* (Matthew 7: 17, 18, 20 emphasis added.)

As a child, I remember the anxious feelings and innocence of expecting good things. I just thought that since I was a good person, good things ought to always happen to me and that bad things only happen to bad people. As I grew to teen years, I became embittered as some of the "bad" things in life began coming my way. It just isn't fair, I thought. Somehow, the whole eternal plan must be frustrated. It wasn't until years later I began to learn that innocence and ignorance expect only good things to happen to them. It takes a greater understanding to realize that the man or woman of Christ expects good to come *from* all things. There is a difference. The apostle Paul understood the difference perfectly when he wrote that: "all things work together for good to them that love God." (Romans 8:28.)

My question then is: if the fruits of my tree (the accident) are good, such as the blessings I received, the love I have felt, the spirit that has presided, the relationships that have been built with the Lord and those I love, the miracles I have experienced, how can the tree be evil? As far as the pain, discomfort, and inconvenience are concerned, one must then ask, "Why are we here on earth?" If pain was never meant to be part of it, then we would be left without the most powerful tool for learning, growth, and change.

My tree of adversity, although young and tender, very soon began to show the signs of a prosperous, fruitful season. Day after day it continues to produce. The cold wind and violent storms of difficult circumstances only seem to nourish and cultivate it, increasing its yield with each season.

The fruits of our struggles are not always immediately evident. The fig tree can take more than six years to bear any kind of fruit at all. Like night follows day, we can be assured that when we are faithful in our suffering, good fruit will always come. It is an immutable law. Some miracles just take time. When the tree of adversity, struggle, and pain produces fruit which is sweet, ripe, and satisfying, I call that a miracle! But, it is a miracle which is promised to all who would walk with honor the long and difficult road of pain.

When we choose to be bitter, hateful, or angry because of our hardships, our tree remains barren and empty. When we choose obedience, praise, and faithful enduring, our trees become laden with the fruit Jesus promised us.

If, in the struggles of our lives, we only focus upon the promises of some future millennial day, then we miss the miracles, growth, and opportunities which stand at our door knocking, here and now. The Lord stands ready to reveal his mighty arm, making the "works of God manifest" in the lives of all who approach him. We do not always get things as we desire them or insist that they should be, but it is my witness that they come as they should, individually wrapped and delivered for our own unique experience and needs. They come, not as obstacles to our happiness and dreams, but as appropriate detours which insure a sweeter victory.

The essence of time in the equation of miracles is paramount to the "works of God being made manifest" in our lives. If we believe that miracles were all meant to be instantaneous, then we deny the very witness of nature itself. While we suffer and seek the "instantaneous" miracle which ensures immediate relief from our suffering, it becomes significant to understand that we do not suffer alone. The Savior has suffered greater than all of us together. He watches his children struggle, weep, and reach upward to him pleading for relief. He must surely desire to give that relief in great abundance, but his perfect love keeps him from instantly alleviating our suffering.

The beauty of a Yosemite Valley or the grandeur of a Grand Canyon all came as a result of the omnipotent hand of the Lord coupled with the ingredient of time. They took hundreds, thousands, maybe even millions of years to create. And what are we left with when the creative process is through? The very epitome of strength, fortitude, wisdom, grandeur, majesty, and awesome glory. No wind, no storm, no lightning or fire can efface their splendor. Nature testifies of the need for the Lord's great power joined with the miracle of time in revealing his almighty arm.

I value the miracle time has brought me more than anything else I can conceive, even more than I would have

171

valued the miracle of walking again, which was promised years ago and which I had hoped would happen immediately. On the day that my limbs receive their natural strength again, I will leap about, dance, run, and shout for joy. But tears will flow freely and my heart will suffer the pain of saying goodbye to my two most cherished and faithful friends, pain and struggle. Time to struggle has brought some of the greatest miracles of all.

The question has been raised to me, "But, Art, what if you never walk again? What if the promises you believe in never become a reality while in this life? How will you feel then?" All very good questions, questions I have already asked, and found answers to. A friend of mine, obviously concerned for my own sense of reality and wanting to protect my feelings, said to me on several occasions, "Art, it's good that you believe you'll walk again in this life, but be careful. Don't put all of your stock in that idea. Live for today; don't dream of intangibles in your tomorrows." I could appreciate his counsel, but on the other hand, he hasn't felt what I have felt and heard what I have heard. I do believe in my tomorrows. One day I will walk again, while in this life.

If life finds me a hundred years old and still sitting in a wheelchair, then I will praise the Lord for giving me that hundred years, and I will rejoice in his perfect plan. My present and future happiness and well-being is not affixed to a dream or a promise. It is firmly seated in the knowledge of an eternal plan which allows for me to someday become as my Father in Heaven. In becoming like him, I will live with him forever. That idea stimulates me and drives me forward. It gives purpose to suffering and hope to pain. Time then becomes my friend as I struggle, learn, grow, and change.

However, if I do live to be a hundred years old and am still in the wheelchair, I will still believe that tomorrow I may walk again, if it is the Lord's plan. Can the clock deny the clockmaker? Can the sculpture resist the hands of the artist? Can the heavens give glory unto themselves? The answers of the universe cry out, "No." All things of worth have their creator. My Father in Heaven designed my spirit, my mother and father worked with him to create my physical body, and today my Savior continues his immortal workings upon my character. All things of worth have their creator. I am not finished yet.

I've often been asked "Art, if you could go back and change it all; if you could have flown a plane, or driven with a different friend, or gone during the daytime, or have loved a different girl in order to have avoided all the pain and suffering you have experienced, would you?"

My answer is simple. "No." To some that may be confusing. Some may not understand, while others may even think I am crazy. But, if they knew what I know and had felt what I have felt, they too would realize that to forfeit pain is to lose all the myriad of miracles, hopes, blessings, and opportunities that go with it. While we walk the stony road we come to a knowledge that it has been trod before by one who has "descended beneath them all" and we experience the priceless blessing of becoming personally acquainted with the Father.

The response of an old man who came across the plains in the ill-fated Martin Handcart Company illustrates my point. He was sitting in a Sunday School class where the teacher was discussing the unfortunate plight of the Saints who were delayed in their journey by early snows as they attempted to reach the Salt Lake Valley by handcart in 1856. In this class the teacher was indulging in some sharp criticism of the Church and its leaders for permitting any company of converts to venture across the plains with no more supplies or protection than a handcart caravan afforded.

It is reported that an old man in the corner sat silent and listened as long as he could stand it, then he arose and said things that no person who heard him will ever forget. His face was white with emotion, yet he spoke calmly, deliberately, but with great earnestness and sincerity.

In substance he said, "I ask you to stop this criticism. You are discussing a matter you know nothing about. Cold historic facts mean nothing here, for they give no proper interpretation of the questions involved. Mistake to send the Handcart Company out so late in the season? Yes. But I was in that company and my wife was in it and Sister Nellie Unthank, whom you have cited, was there, too. We suffered beyond anything you can imagine and many died of exposure and starvation, but did you ever hear a survivor of that company utter a word of criticism? Not one of that company ever apostatized or left the Church, because everyone of us came through with the absolute knowledge that God lives for we became acquainted with him in our extremities.

"I have pulled my handcart when I was so weak and weary from illness and lack of food that I could hardly put one foot ahead of the other. I have looked ahead and seen a patch of sand or a hill slope and I have said, I can go only that far and there I must give up, for I cannot pull the load through it. . . . I have gone on to that sand and when I reached it, the cart began pushing me. I have looked back many times to see who was pushing my cart, but my eyes saw no one. I knew then that the angels of God were there.

"Was I sorry that I chose to come by handcart? No. Neither then nor any minute of my life since. The price we paid to become acquainted with God was a privilege to pay, and I am

174

thankful that I was privileged to come in the Martin Handcart Company." (*Relief Society Magazine*, January 1949, p.8.)

Struggle, pain, miracles, accomplishment, defeat, priesthood power, faith—this has been my story. However, this story is not mine alone. It is the story of every human heart struggling under the weight of life's burdens and learning to find the miracle wrought by time and pain.

Even though, at times, the waves beat against us with unrelenting force and the winds toss us upon the waters, we know that even the strongest storms must end sometime . It is comforting to remember the experience of Peter and the other apostles as they listed on the waves of their storm upon the sea. Peter and the others feared for their lives. All hope appeared to be gone and they felt assured of a watery grave. In their moment of desperation, they turned their eyes to their sleeping Savior, who seemed unconcerned about the waves. With fear in their voices, they awoke the Lord and cried, "Lord, save us: we perish." The Master arose, and the voice of him who created all things stilled the raging waters, "and there was a great calm." (Matthew 8:24-26.)

That same Master who calmed the tempest of the sea also calms my storms and yours. While not always removing the storms from our lives, he replaces fear with faith, and doubt with understanding. In the calm of prayer, we hear his voice. In a recent letter, my mother-in-law included a wonderful testimony which echoes so clearly my own feelings: "How thankful I am that there is something bigger than my fears, and that is the peace that comes from being in that sacred, hallowed place—in the center of his will. That is the only thing that makes life desirable on this earth, that we may attain to that place and more. Then we are able to see the glory of it all more and more—the glory and the end of mortality, our salvation and exaltation. The peace of our God is greater than any of our fears, and that peace is worth the price of our obedience and faithfulness."

Spencer W. Kimball said, "There are depths in the sea which the storms that lash the surface into fury never reach. They who reach down into the depths of life where, in the stillness, the voice of God is heard, have the stabilizing power which carries them poised and serene through the hurricane of difficulties." There is a greater power which stands at the helm of our ships, even in its roughest hours. It's up to us to let him guide us. Only we can relinquish full command to the Perfect One.

Adversity is the common law of life. At some point, we all must stand face to face with despair, discouragement, personal loss, and pain. We sometimes ask the Lord to eliminate these elements of life through the power of the priesthood, not recognizing them as necessary to our final goal. Struggle and pain, as difficult as they may be, are not the enemy. They were not put here to torment or mock men, but to lift and build them.

If we believe that all miracles are instantaneous, mountain-moving experiences of faith, then, when we are left to struggle along our road of pain, it is easy to wonder why the Lord has forgotten us. It can be even more damaging if we think that lack of instantaneous miracles means we lack faith, or that we are less loved by the Lord when divine power isn't immediately rendered to lift us from our circumstances.

To the contrary, the very opposite is true. The Apostle Paul, himself an active participant of adversity, declared, "For whom the Lord loveth he chasteneth, and scourgeth every son whom he receiveth." (Heb. 12:6.) Paul also wrote that, "God is faithful, who will not suffer you to be tempted above that ye are able; but will with the temptation also make a way to escape, that ye may be able to bear it." (1 Cor. 10:13.)

Adversity, pain, and struggle do not challenge the Lord's love for us, they prove it. Likewise, because he has eternally covenanted to give us no struggle or temptation greater than we can bear, the opportunity of time and pain encourage—even require— the growth of our own faith.

To those who love God, the stony, rough way becomes a blessing and an opportunity for miracle after miracle. The rewards are sweeter and the panorama before them more beautiful than the way of ease and instantaneous miracles. When we are denied immediate relief from our heartache, tears, or tragedy, it is because there is a better way that will teach us more and work for our ultimate good. Some miracles just take time. Thank God for that.

Even amidst the light of the ancient miracles and those of today, there is a miracle greater than them all—greater than parting waters, stopping the sun, and healing the sick. The greatest miracle in the world happens every day. The gospel of Jesus Christ works the miracle of change in people's lives.

I know, because the gospel has changed my life. My mission president taught me that I didn't ever have to walk the "low road" again. He taught me that I didn't have to eat the crumbs that fell from the Master's table because my Savior had prepared a feast for me of such a magnitude that I would never hunger again. My life has never been the same.

The gospel changes lives. It changed a young boy in New York into a prophet; a tent-maker into one of the greatest missionaries that ever lived. It changed fishermen into apostles, and it has changed me.

Sitting atop a lonely hill, the Savior asked his disciples whom men thought he was. His disciples answered him saying, "Some say that thou art John the Baptist: some, Elias; and others, Jeremias, or one of the prophets." But then he

177

replied, "But whom say ye that I am?" And Simon Peter answered and said, "Thou art the Christ, the Son of the living God." (Matthew 16:14-16.)

Centuries earlier, Job suffered immeasurable losses. His wealth was stripped from him; his family destroyed. Finally, after all else was gone, he was stricken with boils and failing health. Every day and every hour he suffered physical, emotional, and spiritual pain. His friends mocked him, but Job remained faithful. He emphatically declared, "For I know that my redeemer liveth, and that he shall stand at the latter day upon the earth: And though after my skin worms destroy this body, yet in my flesh I shall see God."(Job 19: 25-26.)

In our day, a young prophet by the name of Joseph Smith, who wore adversity as his daily raiment, bore this solemn witness: "He lives! For we saw him, even on the right hand of God, and we heard the voice bearing record that he is the only Begotten of the Father." (D&C 76:22,23.) A few short years later, Joseph paid the ultimate price for that testimony. He was killed at the hands of a mob with painted faces, betrayed by his second counselor, William Law.

May I humbly, yet solemnly, add my testimony. I know that God lives. I know that Jesus is the Christ. This is his work; this is his church; he stands at the head today. More personally, I testify that he loves his children. When they suffer, whether from the effects of sin or the elements of nature, his perfect heart breaks. Yet his compassionate sorrow for us is swallowed up in his joy at our ultimate victory. For he knows the beginning from the end and sees, even as we suffer, the prize that we will win. There are miracles today. Some miracles just take time. This I believe.

I have found purpose in my suffering. I have been given peace in my understanding. And so, although I do not suggest that I have all of the answers, what answers I do have are sufficient for my happiness right now. And so I continue on, working, trying, struggling, and enjoying the sweet fruit which comes from a tree which is "good."